DUNNE IT
THE HARD WAY

DUNNE IT
THE HARD WAY

The Remarkable Story of a Millwall Legend

Alan Dunne with Chris Davies

First published by Pitch Publishing, 2016

Pitch Publishing
A2 Yeoman Gate
Yeoman Way
Worthing
Sussex
BN13 3QZ

www.pitchpublishing.co.uk

A CIP catalogue record is available for this book from
the British Library.

ISBN 978-1-78531-130-7

Typesetting and origination by Pitch Publishing

Printed by TJ International Ltd, Cornwall, UK

Contents

To mum Elizabeth and dad Paul, my wife Aimee, my two beautiful children Lola and Shay, and not forgetting our little English bulldog Louis.

CHRISTOPHER DAVIES became a Millwall fan aged eight and is happy to be serving a life sentence with no chance of parole. He has worked for the *South London Press*, *Shoot*, the *Daily Star* and, for 20 years, the *Daily Telegraph*. A former chairman of the Football Writers' Association, he is a regular contributor to talkSPORT. He has written a book of his travels, *Behind The Back Page*, edited *Forgive Us Our Press Passes* and, in 2015, *United In Europe* – the most comprehensive book of Manchester United's continental history – was published by Pitch Publishing. Based in Bromley, he is almost as good a cook as he thinks he is and will be friends with anyone who buys him a bottle of Villa Maria Clifford Bay sauvignon blanc.

Acknowledgements

THE BIGGEST influences on my life and career have been my mum Elizabeth, my dad Paul and my wife Aimee. Without their love and encouragement a tearaway teenage Alan Dunne would not have become the captain of Millwall. In fact, I dread to think which course my life could have taken.

My mum died when I was 18 – I think of her and miss her every single day.

I was not the ideal son, but my dad never gave up on me. I wish I had listened to his advice when he told me about the company I was keeping. He took drastic steps to ensure I gave myself the best possible chance of becoming a professional footballer and for that I can never thank him enough.

Aimee, our daughter Lola and our son Shay, are a wonderful, constant reminder that there is something far more important than football.

I served under many managers at The Den but the one who had the most influence on me was Kenny Jackett, so a special thanks to him and for writing the foreword.

Without my Millwall team-mates and the backing of the brilliant Millwall fans my career would not have been so enjoyable, while former chairman Theo Paphitis and current incumbent John Berylson have been incredibly supportive, along with chief executive Andy Ambler, directors James Berylson, Constantine Gonticas, Trevor Keyse, Dernos Kouvaris, Richard Press and Peter Garston. I cannot forget Bob Pearson and Jeff Burnige who were a huge help along the way. And I cannot forget Nicolle Barber and Karen Wilson who have been so good to me.

My friend Tommy Pratt, of Southwark Metals, is a lifelong Millwall fan. Tommy sponsored me during my Lions career, his generosity matched only by the influence of his goldfish that helped us survive relegation *(see chapter 25)*.

Had it not been for the input of Chris Davies this book would not have been possible. I am not sure which he found the more demanding – drinking my coffee or putting my thoughts into words. It was a huge help that Chris is a Millwall supporter and understands what the club are all about.

Thanks mate, pop round for a coffee any time.

A tip of the hat to Steve Clarke and Ken Reynolds for casting a critical eye over the final draft; to Stela Bancheva for research; to Michael Calvin for his help in getting the book up and running; plus Brian Tonks for supplying the photographs of my Millwall career.

Last, but by no means least, thanks to Paul Camillin of Pitch Publishing for enabling this footballer to become an author.

Enjoy.

Foreword By Kenny Jackett

WHEN I came to Millwall in November 2007 they were fourth from bottom in League 1. Dunney writes that I took some time to work him out. Well, that's one way of putting it!

I thought he had a lot of ability and great athleticism for a defender, but needed some direction. All the good things were there, he just had to curb his wild side because he was very competitive.

I think I worked him out okay and he responded well. It was just that his competitiveness at times was counter-productive and he had to channel this into a more positive direction. When he was sent off on his second league start for Leyton Orient he said he never touched the Crawley guy – I've had that conversation with him a few times!

He has a very competitive nature, real fire in his belly, an absolute will to win and to compete. With all this it can be easy to give fouls away and get booked.

The Den is a very emotive place and Millwall fans love a player who shows the spirit and effort demanded. My job…

my challenge…was to restrain Dunney a little while taking nothing away from his incredible desire to win. I loved the raw ingredients he had. I had to teach him to use the high level of competitiveness he always possessed for the benefit of the team.

Alan responded well. He had a lot of natural ability and once he rounded off the edges, harnessing the many good assets he had and controlling the competitive nature, he turned into a well-disciplined professional very quickly and gave the club many outstanding performances.

When I first knew him he was quite quiet, but I felt he had enough personality to help other people and influence the team. He had a decent understanding of rights and wrongs as a player and person. Dunney knew when the lads were out of order and when they had stepped out of line.

This grew to such an extent that he eventually became Millwall captain, which I always felt would happen naturally as he became older. I cannot say this was all down to me, but it was good to hear that Dunney has said so many nice things about me in his book. I do appreciate that.

Dunney wasn't always a popular figure with the supporters, but had perseverance and Millwall fans love someone who fights back, which he did. If things weren't going well for him or the side, his response was always to dig in, get his tackles in and pass the ball positively which really helps. When a side is having a bad run, you need leaders…people with determination to put on a performance that can turn things round.

He has an incredible ability, guts and determination to battle and reprove himself which he's shown on many occasions. Millwall fans really took to him for that.

I remember one game in particular during my last year when Millwall played Crystal Palace, who went on to be promoted shortly after this match. He had Wilfried Zaha in his pocket. The draw went a long way to helping us to stay up in the Championship – Dunney certainly played his part, not just against Palace but the whole season.

Off the field I know he is devoted to his wife Aimee and his kids Lola and Shay. Everything centres around them, which I find quite admirable. Believe it or not he was, to some degree, rather shy initially, but I always knew there was a shrewd football brain there and as Dunney has got older this has developed.

I believe Alan has the ability to become a good coach or manager. He has the football brain, the personality and the confidence. Coaching is brains and Dunney has what it takes to influence people effectively.

Dunney never quite made the Republic of Ireland team. I know he was very close and was consistent enough to do a job for them. In recent years they have had Seamus Coleman and Stephen Kelly, who both had Premier League experience, as right-back options so the competition was fierce.

Could I go head-to-head with him as a manager one day? I hope to stay around as long as I can while Dunney is still playing.

Never say never.

KENNY JACKETT
Millwall manager
November 2007 – May 2013.

1

Told I was no longer wanted at Millwall over a beer

I considered playing in India

NEIL HARRIS handed me a beer though there was nothing to celebrate. 'Dunney,' he said. 'It's bad news.'

In fact, it could hardly have been worse. And it was to lead to the toughest two months of my career.

He continued, 'The club have decided you need a change. It was a difficult decision to make, but next season Shaun Cummings will be the first-choice right-back, Sid Nelson will play centre-half.

'You might not be playing and I don't think you'd want to be here if you are not getting games. You're the sort of person who needs to play.'

Relegation from the Championship at the end of 2014/15 guaranteed significant changes at Millwall, with finance dictating many decisions. Yet when Harris called me in his office I believe I had every reason to be hopeful it was to discuss a new deal rather than my departure from the only club I had played for.

I told Harris I wanted to stay, to help the team, especially the young lads, in League 1 because they would need someone with my experience. I had also never been one to go knocking on the manager's door each time I was dropped.

My attitude had always been to get my head down, not make waves and try to win back my place…which on many occasions I had to do.

Harris and I had been team-mates for a number of years and we became friends. He admitted telling me the news was 'tough…difficult…the hardest thing I'd had to do' but he felt I could still play in the Championship and would give any interested manager a glowing report about me.

In the end, I was happy to drop two divisions and sign for Leyton Orient of League 2.

I know it wasn't easy for Harris, who had been there for me over the years, giving me a lot of good advice. I have much respect for the Millwall legend and I would never have wanted a new contract as a favour – not that he would have done this.

If a new deal was going to be put on the table, it must only have been because the manager felt it was best for the club. Harris made the decision and if he believed I was surplus to requirements I respected that.

However, I was in shock. While no one from the side could take much credit from a season that ended in relegation, I had played in 42 matches – more than any other outfield player.

I felt I deserved at least the offer of another contract.

I realised I would have had to take a drop in salary though money has never been a huge motivating factor for me and there have been quite a few players at The Den who have earned two or three times what I did. I was still happy at Millwall who had been very good to me over the years.

My future seemed to have been decided in one day, though perhaps I'll never really know.

I think it was the wrong decision for the club to make, though I accepted it even if I believed I still had more to offer.

The day when I left Millwall was always going to come – I just didn't think it would be when and how it did. I didn't feel my time at The Den was up, I thought there would be another year.

John Berylson, the chairman, once said to me, 'I hope you retire in a Millwall shirt.' That was my dream, but how many people's dreams come true? Life isn't like that and you cannot write your own script.

My dad, Paul, said, 'You haven't left Millwall…you are just going for now, it's a temporary parting.'

It was not a divorce, only a separation.

✳   ✳   ✳   ✳   ✳

MILLWALL'S relegation had been confirmed before the final game of 2014/15, a 4-2 away defeat to Wolves. As I walked off the pitch at Molineux I had no idea it was to be my last match for the club I had been with for 23 years.

I was boarding the coach when I saw Mark McGhee, Gordon Strachan's assistant with Scotland, and I shouted over to him. We had a brief chat about the game and shared a few memories. It was good to see McGhee who had given me my debut 13 years earlier so he had witnessed my first and last matches for Millwall.

The next day was the end of season awards party where I spoke to a couple of board members who gave no indication I would not be with Millwall the following year.

My contract was ending in June and while there had been no talks about a new deal, the signs were positive, not least because on the Tuesday the players who had been told they were being kept on had to report for a fitness test, to assess things like weight and body fat which would be checked when pre-season training began.

I had been instructed to be there though Harris was not present because he was involved in a meeting with the board. That night I played in the first half of a charity match along with Harris.

At half-time Chopper said he wanted to see me in his office to give me what turned out to be the worst news of my career.

✳   ✳   ✳   ✳   ✳

I RETURNED home almost in tears and told my daughter Lola who was a few days shy of her ninth birthday what had happened. She started crying and my wife, Aimee, had a go at me for telling Lola.

I felt I needed to share the news with my family and there is no easy way to pass on sad times.

Not the best day in the life of Alan Dunne.

The following day we all went on holiday to Dubai where, for the first two nights, I could not sleep. I kept going over and over what had happened and why it had happened, but maybe you can over-think things at times.

John Berylson tried to contact me, but I wasn't ready to talk to anyone. As he was probably in Boston it would have cost me £2 a minute for a transatlantic call so I texted him and said, 'Chairman, I'll ring you when I get home,' which I did.

I thanked him for all he had done for me and he was very complimentary, hoping one day I'd return in a coaching capacity.

'The door is always open for you, Alan,' he said. 'You'll always be welcome back.'

My phone was almost on meltdown and not just because of the heat in Dubai.

It was humbling that directors, other players and friends in football texted me. Sid Nelson and Ben Thompson were just two of the younger lads who tweeted nice things about me which meant a lot.

*   *   *   *   *

'ALL GREAT changes are preceded by chaos.'

This was a message my wife, Aimee, texted me. At the time, I had no idea what the next step in my career would be, but I can look back on my time at Millwall with a million happy memories.

I achieved just about everything I could reasonably have expected, apart from playing in the Premier League which was always going to be very difficult. If the supporters see me as a Millwall legend, that fills me with pride. It was all I ever wanted to be as a kid and I know my mum, Elizabeth, looking down on me, would also be so proud.

I played for the club I love for 23 years and for that I am thankful. I was part of an FA Cup Final squad, I was voted Player of the Year, I won the Goal of the Year award, I played at Wembley in an FA Cup semi-final and a play-off final. I experienced European football while I was also appointed captain. The club granted me a testimonial and I played 388 games for Millwall, scoring 23 goals.

I miss The Den – I remain a Millwall fan and my heart will always be with the Lions. I met some wonderful people during my time there and as much as anything it was disappointing not to be able to say a proper thank-you to the tremendous Millwall fans when I left.

That day will come. But when I look back on my 23 years with Millwall I am left with one big regret.

2

I should have asked Millwall for a transfer

It was the only way I could have got a new contract

THE BIGGEST regret of my career is not asking Millwall for a transfer soon after the start of 2014/15. At the end of the previous campaign, when we beat Bournemouth in the final game to avoid relegation, I had a year remaining on my contract.

When I went to see Ian Holloway about a new deal his first words were, 'Because of you we have stayed up…I can't thank you enough. You are one of the most honest people I've met in the game.'

While I may have earned decent money, I was receiving nowhere near the salaries of the best-paid players at the club. I had captained the team in the successful run-in to safety, enjoying my role in the centre of defence. I asked the gaffer if I could have a new contract that at least gave me something like parity with those at the top of the pay scale.

Ollie told me he had other contracts to sort out 'but you'll get your turn…I'll look after you and sort it out'.

When we reported back for pre-season his mood had changed. 'We just want to see those seven or eight games weren't a fluke,' he said. 'We want to see that you can play centre-half but Dunney, trust me, you'll get your turn.'

We started the season with a 2-0 win over Leeds at The Den before beating Fulham 1-0 at Craven Cottage. A draw away to Sheffield Wednesday was followed by a 1-0 home defeat by Rotherham, but a 2-1 victory over Blackpool saw Millwall top of the Championship at the end of August.

At that moment I regret not being selfish. I put the club first instead of handing in a transfer request. This was the only way, I believe, that I would have got what I wanted.

I was captain, Millwall were top of the league, I like to think I had shown my form of four months earlier was no fluke. I should have said, 'Give me a new contract or I want to leave.'

Had I done that I am confident I would have been given a new two-year deal with my wages increased. I can't see how the club would have said no given how we had hit the ground running.

There were players earning far more than me without playing anything like the number of games I had or given as much as I had for the club.

I feel they wanted me to see out my existing deal and if all went well, they could offer me a new contract. Of course, Holloway's dismissal and relegation changed everything.

I am very grateful for what I have, but when a footballer is approaching the end of his career memories don't pay the bills.

So why didn't I go through with the transfer request? I was confident the club would look after me, but it backfired.

I never thought Holloway would be sacked mid-season. Had he kept his job I am sure he would have seen I was given what I deserved.

A two-year contract would have taken me to the end of 2017/18 when I would have been within touching distance of my 36th birthday. Chances are I would have retired having spent my entire career with Millwall, which had always been an ambition, and found a different role at the club.

When I look back, the moral is if you are in the driving seat, take advantage of this position. Strike while the iron's hot.

A footballer has to look after himself and if you think that is being disloyal, clubs do not always respect or reward loyalty.

* * * * *

MY CONTRACT with Millwall officially ended on 30 June 2015. Like many others inside and outside football, I was unemployed. I seek no sympathy because it is part of the game in the lower leagues, but the stress of waiting for someone to call me with the right offer was a new and unwelcome experience.

While I never thought my phone would be constantly ringing, I had made 42 appearances for Millwall the previous season and could fit in anywhere across the back four. I was hopeful my future would be sorted out pretty quickly.

I was wrong. Two months after being told I would not be retained by Millwall, I was still without a club.

Every message or call I received I thought 'yes, this could be it' and I was almost disappointed when it was 'only' a mate.

There was nothing I could do; I was not in control of my own destiny…that was in the hands of others, though I had no idea who they might be. I could not go seeking employment or looking for a new club – clubs had to come to me.

All clubs have a list of players available on a free transfer and perhaps they wait until a week or two into pre-season to see how their squad is shaping up…which positions they may need to strengthen for the upcoming campaign.

I maintained a strict training regime in the gym plus, of course, pounding the pavements. I gave it all my usual enthusiasm and dedication.

It was essential that while I had not played any pre-season matches, my general fitness, which has always been good, was as sharp as it could be. Of course I missed going to a training ground and joining in the chit-chat – it was the first time I had never started a new season in the traditional way.

Yet I was not alone in waiting for my phone to ring with some good news because around 700 players are released by English clubs each summer. I had been lucky to have enjoyed such a memorable career with Millwall.

By the age of 21, 75 per cent of professional footballers have moved away from the pro game.

❋   ❋   ❋   ❋   ❋

I CAN only speculate why I had a summer of discontent. Maybe managers were looking for more youthful sides, then when the season starts they realise the kids need an older hand to provide experience.

Perhaps some thought I was typecast having been with Millwall so long and would not be able to play as consistently for another club. To a certain extent I can understand that, but any club who had done their homework on me would have realised this was not the case.

The worry of not knowing where – of even if – I would kick off the new season caused arguments between Aimee and I. For example, I was told Blackpool were interested.

We sat down and talked about whether Aimee and our children, Lola and Shay, would move there. It would mean changing their schools. Would Aimee stay in our Beckenham home and I'd find a flat in Blackpool, coming back whenever I could?

We talked and talked – and I heard no more from Blackpool.

It was a similar situation with Crewe and Hearts. Contact was made, hopes built up, more discussions with Aimee…I was actually on my way to Crewe when I received a call to say there was an imminent change in their backroom staff and the trial game I was due to play in had been cancelled.

I turned round and went back home.

In my mind, I was also having problems letting go of Millwall. I would have re-signed for them for the money any of these clubs had mentioned.

True, there was no point in looking back at the disappointment of being released by Millwall. That was history. We cannot change the past and it was better to channel all my energies into preparing for the next step in my career.

Easier said than done.

While they meant well, it didn't help when friends and people in football were constantly phoning me asking how things were going. I went to watch Bromley play Millwall pre-season and the response from the fans was incredible, asking, 'Why did they let you go?'

It was heart-warming, though in some ways only added to my frustration.

* * * * *

I THOUGHT about playing in the Indian Super League which has eight franchises, the season running from September to December. David Platt, Nicolas Anelka, Peter Taylor, Roberto Carlos and Zico were among the coaches. I started to follow a couple of teams on Twitter and before I knew it hundreds of Indian fans were saying how much they were looking forward to seeing me out there.

In the end I decided to hang on in England and I was happy to sign a two-year contract with Leyton Orient on 27 July.

Orient are regarded by many London supporters as their unofficial second club. They have always had a good, popular image and when I met manager Ian Hendon and his assistant Andy Hessenthaler I believed Orient were a club I would enjoy playing for. It also meant no disruption for my family.

I had the first medical of my career, which was a little unusual. I then walked into the Orient dressing room and all the lads looked at the new boy…a situation I'd experienced many times with Millwall, but I knew a few of them so the banter soon started.

As I signed the contract everything felt right. It was all very different to what I had been used to, but a challenge I was relishing.

One of the first things I told the manager was that I wanted to help Orient win promotion back to League 1.

Orient was a whole new world for me, but something I wanted to embrace.

Perhaps it helped when I pulled on the Orient shirt for the first time in a friendly against Woking that it was blue, the second strip.

I had to programme my head to say, 'I'm a winner. Whichever shirt I wear I want to win, whether it's Millwall or Leyton Orient.'

I was also aware that I had to stop referring to Millwall as 'we' or 'us'. It was like learning another language. Millwall will always be part of me, but how many players play for the club they support? Very few. That does not mean you cannot give another club the same as you gave the one you were brought up with.

You can grow to love another club, as Jamie Carragher, a boyhood Everton fan, did with Liverpool. I now support two teams: Leyton Orient and Millwall.

✳ ✳ ✳ ✳ ✳

IAN HENDON is an old-school manager, which I like, and I respected that he was happy to give me a two-year contract.

You would be amazed at the number of players who sign for a club and then tell their new team-mates, 'The club's shit and the manager's a wanker.'

They are paying him his wages for the next two, three or four years, regardless of form or injury, his salary is guaranteed, and yet the guy who brought him there is a wanker. Amazing.

Such an attitude is so unprofessional. I respect any manager who has effectively given me a job and my family security.

In return, I gave my utmost for him whether I was in the team or not until his departure in January, 2016.

*　*　*　*　*

ONE OF my first decisions after signing for Leyton Orient was my shirt number. The kit man Ada Martin, known as 'Meat Loaf' because he's a real dead ringer for the rock singer, offered me numbers three, four or five.

I didn't fancy three because it is traditionally worn by a left-back, a position I would only play in an emergency. Number four? No, that's for a midfielder. I opted for number five.

It was strange signing my first autograph as an Orient player 'Alan Dunne 5' after being 'Alan Dunne 2' for so long.

*　*　*　*　*

WHEN I joined Leyton Orient the impression I had was that my new team-mates and the backroom staff saw me as a cross between Vinnie Jones and Joey Barton.

Their perception, no doubt based on my Millwall disciplinary record and reputation, was that Alan Dunne was not a man to upset. Don't rub Dunney up the wrong way or you will live to regret it.

I had no idea this was how others saw me and I found it a little scary and embarrassing. It was like, 'Oh God, look, he's wearing studs in training, please don't smash me.'

My former team-mate Scott Barron pointed out that I had been captain of Millwall, a club with a certain stigma. My status of who I was and how I played gave me a reputation in the eyes of others – an image to be feared, almost.

True, I have always trained and played hard, to the maximum, but I hope off the pitch I am more of a gentleman than a bad boy.

I should have asked Millwall for a transfer

In my first month with Orient I took a water bottle into the treatment room without thinking that this meant a £10 fine. A couple of young players noticed this, yet it was a case of 'you tell him', 'no YOU tell him, I'm not going to do it'.

On the coach returning from an early away trip I got up to make myself a cup of coffee and Dean Cox said to one of the young lads, 'Sit down, someone make him a coffee...NOW.'

I also spotted two bags of crisps on a seat, not realising they were Cox's. I opened one packet and asked if anyone wanted a crisp. The lads looked to Coxey to see what he was going to do and he said, 'Fuck that, I'm not telling him.'

On the away trip to Exeter in August 2015, as a new boy I had to sing a song after dinner the night before the match. I chose 'Mack The Knife' by Bobby Darin which reached number one in 1959. I accept that my version was shit, though I don't think it should be blamed for our 4-0 defeat the following day.

As I started to sing – or attempt to sing – the mobiles came out. I stopped and said, 'If any of you fuckers put this on social media...'

I didn't have to finish the sentence. I've never seen so many phones go back into pockets so quickly.

3

Confident Ollie wanted to change the bonus system

But did he really believe we could push for promotion?

A WEEK before the 2014/15 season began Ian Holloway called the seniors – me, Danny Shittu, Carlos Edwards and David Forde – into his office to discuss our bonuses with Millwall chief executive Andy Ambler.

Under the existing agreement, players were paid out on positions one to six, seven to 12 and 13 to 20 in the 24-club Championship. If we were in the bottom four we got nothing.

Ollie wanted to scrap all the bonuses from seventh to 20th while maximising the one to six payments. He was confident that the squad he had was good enough to be in the top six and so no bonus should be awarded for any other position.

I'm not sure whether Ollie really believed the squad was that strong or if it was a clever bit of management mind-games in an effort to keep us in the promotion hunt. Though I liked his positive thinking, I did not agree that with the current squad we would be a top six side and as a result the players would lose many potential bonuses.

I spoke up, which may have been a bit daring, to air my views and said: 'With what we have at the moment, I don't think it's enough.' The look on Ollie's face was one of pure shock and surprise.

My opinion was greeted by silence though I felt, as captain, it should, rightly or wrongly, be shared within the four walls.

Eventually, we agreed to keep the bonus payments down to 20th place, but with less money for being below sixth.

✳   ✳   ✳   ✳   ✳

SADLY, my instincts were proved correct. We just didn't have the quality needed to compete in the Championship and Millwall endured another season of struggle.

You can give everything for the shirt but when you are simply not good enough then effort alone cannot compensate for the level of talent required. If you hand even the best managers a poor team there is little they can do.

The chairman backed Ian Holloway which was the right decision because I thought that the manager would eventually get it right. When Ollie arrived expectations were high because of what he had done at other clubs, fans believing there would be an immediate turnaround. This was unrealistic though I maintain it was the players rather than the manager who were to blame for Millwall's poor form.

Many people who spoke to me said Holloway made too many changes with team selection, tactics and formations – altering the system far too early during matches. This meant the way we played was changing not just from game to game, but even in the first half of some matches.

My view was you had to respect a guy who had led two teams – Blackpool and Crystal Palace – to promotion to the Premier League, but at Millwall perhaps his approach was too complicated for the players and the fans to comprehend.

Being captain, I felt I had let the gaffer down because the side were involved in another relegation battle which really disappointed me.

As we fought against the drop, some players were playing for themselves rather than the team, having their own agendas instead of sacrificing everything for the good of the club. They would try Hollywood shots from 30 yards, hoping for headlines when they should have passed to a team-mate in a better position.

They would over-compensate going forward to look impressive, putting personal glory top of their priority list.

It is too simple to say 'just tell them'. First of all, they would be in denial while in-fighting affects team spirit. But when contracts are running down and futures are uncertain, players tend to do what is best for them and look after their individual needs. However, every player was still being paid by Millwall and should have served the club accordingly. It doesn't work like that, though. Millwall had too many people earning vast sums of money who did not put the club first.

They were greedy individuals who only cared about getting their pay cheque and did not have the passion or love for the club that is a basic requirement.

✳   ✳   ✳   ✳   ✳

MIDWAY THROUGH 2014/15 I was drained. Not tired as I was still physically as fit as ever even though the Championship is a long, hard slog. But three years on the bounce of fighting relegation was taking its toll.

There had been far too many lows and very few highs as Millwall again found themselves in a battle against the drop.

Off the field, there was the worry of being in the final year of my contract coupled with the inevitable abuse you receive when you are near the bottom of the table.

Mentally this affects you and I was relieved to be left out of the side on occasions to recharge my batteries. People might point out that Cristiano Ronaldo and Lionel Messi play 90 minutes of every game, but when you are winning most weeks and have no concerns about your next contract life is much easier.

I realise I am fortunate to earn a decent living and for that I am grateful. But to train hard, put everything into every match and not get the rewards has a negative effect on you after a while.

Also, in my head I felt I was a central defender and not a modern-day right-back. I could not get up and down as I used to when I was in my early 20s. Because of injuries I found myself playing mostly in my 'old' role or occasionally left centre-half. While I would always give 100 per cent, in the back of my mind I was being used in a position in which I no longer felt confident.

Ian Holloway wouldn't accept this because he believed a defender should be able to play anywhere along the back line though I was switched back to a central role in February.

As much as anything, when you are losing week in, week out it affects your confidence, regardless of what level you play. I was going to bed thinking about what was going wrong and what could be done to rectify this.

I had been down Worry Road many times and I was good at bouncing back. Millwall brought in sports psychologists and while some players may find them helpful, they didn't work for me. I sat there thinking, 'You don't really know me.'

My wife and my dad are my most important 'sports psychologists', particularly my dad because he has known me from day one.

Strange as it may sound, I am best when I have my back to the wall. Too many pats on the head make me feel uncomfortable. I seem to react when people start to doubt me. The chairman always used to tell me, 'You're a fighter,' and he was right.

Even when Millwall were struggling, I still loved playing football. I get knocked down, I get up again. I can't feel sorry for myself as I am paid good money to go out there and put it right. I do something millions – no, billions – love to do and I count myself fortunate.

Whenever my emotions take a dive I soon snap out of it.

MILLWALL had narrowly escaped relegation the two previous seasons so the drop at the end of 2014/15 was hardly a big surprise. We had not done enough good business in the transfer windows, instead bringing in players who were not up to the required standard. There were too many loan players, but more than anything, there were too few goals in the team.

We had 15 clean sheets, which would normally see a team finish around mid-table. With scoring so difficult, our goals against tally was not enough for Millwall to survive.

The club can rebuild and go again, though since 2004 when the Championship was rebranded only six of the 30 teams relegated were promoted from League 1 the following season.

As 2015/16 started there was a new wave of optimism at The Den with Harris starting his first full campaign as the manager. Millwall went down to League 1 in 2006 and it was four years before the club returned to the Championship. Fingers crossed it is quicker this time round.

I doubt if my time with Leyton Orient will match my Millwall career which was a roller-coaster ride of highs and lows, while the journey had more than its share of aches and pains.

4

Fights, bites and kicking team-mates

I learned my lesson the hard way

THE FIRE EXTINGUISHER crashed against the back of my head. Punches and kicks rained in all over my body as I curled up to defend myself the best I could. One of the assailants bit my lower lip, causing an injury that required a dozen or so stitches.

As I lay there helpless, I remember saying to myself, 'Please don't stab me…no knives…no knives…please don't stab me.' It was some consolation no blades were used on me, just fists, a foot and teeth.

And a fire extinguisher.

I was 17 and in a nightclub called Bon Bonnes in Herne Hill, south-east London, with former Millwall defender Jamie Stuart and others. Some would say not the best of company considering he had been sacked by Charlton Athletic after testing positive for cocaine and cannabis and banned by the Football Association for six months.

But this was typical of the way I lived at the time. I was strutting around like I'd played 300 league games; a Millwall player with an inflated opinion of my own importance.

I bumped into a guy – or he bumped into me, take your pick – while I was chatting to a girl I knew. I think he was a little jealous I was talking to her and after an exchange of less than friendly words I was not just fighting him, I was dragged into the kitchen area where two or three of his mates piled in on me.

If I was not a totally innocent party, I certainly did not deserve the going-over I received.

Eventually – I have no real recollection of time – some security guards heard the commotion and forced their way in. I was taken to King's College Hospital in an ambulance and it is stating the obvious to say I was in agony. My bottom lip was almost hanging off.

The police were called, but I had no memory of what the thugs looked like. It was dark and within seconds I was curled up on the floor. Nobody else knew who they were and no names were put forward so no charges were brought.

I had to go into training the next morning and explain to manager Mark McGhee I had been beaten up in a nightclub. I thought about lying and saying I was mugged.

I had made up a story to cover up what really happened. When I went in to see the manager I changed my mind at the last second. I am not really sure why, probably because I realised that if I was caught lying it would make the situation much, much worse.

It could even have been the end for me at Millwall.

I felt it was better to be honest and take whatever punishment the club may have handed me. As it was, they were sympathetic, but it was a black mark against my name.

Given the beating I sustained, I was fortunate to miss only one reserve game.

If there was any good to come out of being kicked like a football, it was the wake-up call I needed and a harsh, painful lesson was learned. My dad had continually warned me about the company I was keeping.

From that day, if I was ever in a nightclub or bar, I always stood with my back to the wall, keeping myself to myself and not becoming involved with anyone about anything.

It took a serious beating for the penny to drop, but since then nothing like this has occurred again.

❊　❊　❊　❊　❊

THERE has always been a drinking culture in English football, though it has slowed down a little from the Eighties when a lager-fest and a fight among team-mates was part of Liverpool's pre-match build-up.

For most clubs during the 1960s, 70s and 80s having a few pints after training was accepted. It was almost mandatory. Beer was regarded as all right because there was a lot of water in it, so I heard.

Football's awareness of what players should (and should not) eat and drink has changed considerably, though the danger of too much alcohol remains.

These days, young players who may be single with no baggage have a lot of time on their hands and it is easy to be sucked into going to the wrong places in the afternoon or on days off. Earlier in my career I was no different and while I have learned my lesson – well, several lessons – the temptations for players in their late teens and early 20s, particularly, are still there.

My hope is that any young player reading this may learn from the mistakes I made.

In the 2012/13 season there was a disturbing pattern of excessive drinking, two or three nights a week, with some senior professionals who had made their money and younger players who had yet to play a game all being drawn into the fake glamour of the West End nightlife.

But who was I to give my opinion after I had been in the same situation which almost cost me my career?

When I was younger, some older players would invite me to drinking sessions and in my inexperienced eyes I thought it would look good if I was seen with them. It was like earning a shady brownie point.

The secret is to do everything in moderation, though that is much easier to say than carry through. I remember one Millwall player who found it impossible to control his drinking.

He was still under the influence during a game.

After coming on as a substitute during a cup tie on a Tuesday night at The Den he scored and it was only then his boozy secret was revealed.

As team-mates ran to congratulate him the smell of alcohol on his breath was evident. In the dressing room following the match he was pulled aside by the other players and told in no uncertain terms that he was lucky he had scored.

Had he not scored and been a liability in a defeat he would probably have been reported to the manager.

There is an argument that we should have done this regardless of his goal, but it was decided to give him a second chance. He was a young centre-forward and I hoped he had learned his lesson.

Sadly not, because in April 2015 Chris Zebroski, then with Newport County, was jailed for four years and four months after admitting four charges of robbery, attempted robbery and assault relating to two incidents.

Zebroski, who said he was 'a bit over the [alcohol] limit', had his contract immediately terminated by the Welsh club.

* * * * *

GLAZED eyes at the training ground are not an uncommon sight in English football while hangovers can be run off. Playing while still on an alcoholic high is a different matter entirely.

An occasional social drink can help a player unwind, though if this becomes a regular habit his form is bound to suffer.

Also, in this age of mass social media and where every mobile phone has a camera facility there is no hiding place for players and clubs tend to know of any excesses very quickly.

* * * * *

ONE OF MY good pals, Lenny Pidgeley, was at Millwall between 2005 and 2009 and in 2006/07 he was our first-choice goalkeeper. The following season saw the arrival of Kenny Jackett in November 2007 and two days before he joined the club Pidgeley, Zak Whitbread and I went up the West End for a drink or two. Afterwards, we returned to Pidgeley's flat in Beckenham where Whitbread, who'd had one too many, thought it would be funny to two-foot Lenny's new cream coloured carpet with his black shoes while he was in the toilet.

Hilarious at the time for us, but as Pidgeley came out of the bathroom he was not amused when he saw black footmarks all over his living room carpet. With the earlier consumption of Grey Goose vodka kicking in, an aggressive exchange of words led to Pidgeley losing his temper and punching Whitbread, breaking his nose and putting his head through the plasterboard wall. There was blood everywhere and things escalated to a level where it was difficult for me to separate them.

It sounds ridiculous to say they were good mates, but they were.

The next morning the physio patched Whitbread up the best he could. The following day, Jackett's first in charge, the new manager was greeted by a defender who looked like something out of *Spitting Image*, a goalkeeper who had done a passable imitation of Mike Tyson and a right-back who was guilty by association.

Fair play to Jackett who said, 'It's a fresh start from today. I don't want to know what happened on Tuesday night. I'm only concerned with what happens from today onwards.'

But I knew in Jackett's mind that Pidgeley had no future at Millwall.

He soon joined Woking on loan before signing for Carlisle United.

Jackett did not like players going out drinking and particularly dreaded Christmas parties which have given football too many negative headlines over the years. If he heard about a social evening, I could sense that he just wanted it over and done with. He felt anything more than downing a couple of beers was disrespecting the job.

* * * * *

MY MOST stupid association with alcohol came as I celebrated my 24th birthday.

I had bought a flash new car which I wanted to drive everywhere, even to the Epping Forest Country Club in Essex for my birthday celebrations. I was not aware of having a lot to drink – it was far from being a heavy session – though of course one beer is one too many when you are driving.

The police car coming from the other direction passed me and turned around to follow me. They flashed their lights and I pulled over.

I was told I was driving too fast, though the V6 engine on the Porsche Cayenne probably attracted their attention as much as anything – if not the pink T-shirt I was wearing.

I guess I was asking for trouble and as soon as I was stopped I knew what was coming. I was right.

The roadside breath test showed me over the limit. At Bexleyheath Police Station I was questioned and re-breathalysed. It measured 53 – the legal limit is 35 microgrammes per 100 millilitres of breath. I felt ashamed and when I telephoned Aimee to tell her where I was in the early hours of the morning, she rightly gave me the hairdryer treatment, repeating that she had warned me about the dangers of drinking and driving.

The next morning – correction, later that morning – I had to apologise to the club and fortunately the incident did not make the papers. I pleaded guilty to the offence by post rather than appear in court and I was handed the mandatory 12-month ban which included a six-week alcohol awareness course in Kingston-upon-Thames in south-west London every second Sunday.

Not the easiest of train journeys, but all part of the punishment.

Some of the things I saw on the course horrified me, making me wonder how on earth I could have done something as dangerous as driving under the influence of alcohol. They showed explicit photographs of drink-drive crashes with cars turned upside down and the fire brigade cutting people out of vehicles.

The course comprised a mixed bag from society; a teacher, a solicitor, a grandfather, a few mums plus me, a random footballer. We bonded, different people brought together by a single reckless act.

What I was told and what I learned on the course had a profound effect on me. I was just grateful no one was harmed by my irresponsibility and it goes without saying that since then, if I ever have a drink the car stays at home.

Apart from the £700 fine that came with the ban, I spent a small fortune on taxis going to and from training – there is a limit on how many favours you can call up. I still had to pay £600 a month for the car under the lease agreement.

I got what I deserved and if anybody is ever tempted to drive after a few beers I have one word of advice.

Don't.

5

I had to pay a player's dental bill after head-butt

And the club fined me a week's wages

A PROFESSIONAL footballer has to make some social sacrifices, whether he is an England international with a top Premier League club or a League 2 hopeful.

It is easy, but unrealistic to say footballers should not drink, though whatever your job, there should be no excesses. A few beers or a couple of glasses of wine occasionally can be a welcome escape from the stresses of the sport – we all need to switch off now and again.

Believe me, I've done it both ways.

As Millwall captain I felt I had more of a responsibility to the younger players, particularly, and to impress upon them that quantity does matter – the amount they might put away on a night out is likely to affect them for a few days afterwards.

For a couple of years when I was a teenager, football was not my priority, but I do not think it is hypocritical to preach what I did not always practise. It wasn't that long ago I was one of them and I hoped others could learn and benefit from my experiences and mistakes.

Young players should enjoy themselves and have fun, but not at the expense of their football.

Alcohol affects people in different ways. Some believe they are the next Frank Sinatra or Kanye West, no major problem there. Some become over-friendly, telling you they want to marry you – just say no. The trouble comes when alcohol makes you wind people up to an unacceptable level which I have witnessed too many times.

A few years ago I remember an incident between Neil Harris and Marvin Elliott when we were on a night out in T.G.I. Friday's. Chopper was 'over-happy' and Elliott's shirt was suddenly covered in sauce. In response Elliott squirted some back in Chopper's face.

It escalated and Harris grabbed Elliott by his now-stained shirt and in doing so broke the new £700 chain that was around his neck.

The pair had to be pulled apart and inevitably Dennis Wise, who was manager at the time, got to hear about it. At the next training session, as we prepared for our warm-up, Wisey placed four poles about 15 feet apart and taped them up like a boxing ring. While the rest of us went to loosen up, he told Chopper and Elliott, 'Get in the ring and sort out your problems.'

He added, 'You can talk, fight, whatever, just get it sorted.'

When we had finished our first lap the pair were hugging each other and laughing. We all started bantering them, let's say doubting their masculinity…after taking their so-called gloves off they were lovey-dovey which left the pair open to remarks best not repeated here.

It will probably not surprise you to learn that my confrontations have not always ended with a cuddle.

* * * * *

A PARTICULARLY regrettable altercation with a team-mate was at a Millwall pre-season friendly away to Dartford soon after Kenny Jackett took over. I was desperate to impress the manager and I felt during the game Mark Laird was guilty of an error that made it look like it was my mistake as the Dartford winger broke free.

I was livid and my mood did not change while we were warming down after the match. When I told Laird of his mistake his response was sarcastic, inferring that I was stupid.

I lost it and head-butted him.

Some fans were still hanging around and they witnessed what happened. I think there were a couple of mentions on social media, but thankfully it did not make any headlines.

I was totally out of order. What I did was indefensible. I immediately said I was sorry, but I don't blame Laird for not accepting my apology at the time. If someone had done it to me, I would have felt the same. I have no excuses for my irresponsible and dangerous act of violence.

The club fined me a week's wages and I had to pay his dental bill because one of his teeth had become loose.

I have no complaints about this and to add to my punishment, my wife gave me the third degree when I told her what had happened.

It is little consolation to Laird that I have subsequently learned to control my temper a lot better. Not totally, but the immediate rush of blood to the head is a thing of the past.

*   *   *   *   *

I SEEM TO have been involved in incidents with players who were to become Millwall team-mates. Shortly before Richard Shaw joined the club from Coventry in 2006, we played the Sky Blues and I stood on his foot as we waited for a corner to be taken.

Shaw didn't react. It was as if nothing had happened. Good pro, he wasn't going to fall for that one.

When he signed for Millwall he joked, 'You still want to fight me, Dunney?'

'No way.'

In February 2013 we won 2-1 at Middlesbrough, both sides desperate for points. Boro had a late potential equaliser by Scott McDonald, who was to later join Millwall, ruled out for offside. I saw the assistant's flag go up and within seconds the referee, Michael Naylor, was surrounded by home players trying to convince him the goal was good.

Ever the peacemaker, I tried to protect the official, telling the Boro players to fuck off and that the decision was correct, advising them to leave Naylor alone. Nicky Bailey, who became a Millwall team-mate, pushed me in the face as I pulled him away from the ref who did not see this with so much going on. I could understand Bailey's frustration because Boro were heading for their sixth consecutive defeat and the disallowed goal was virtually the last kick of the game.

Bailey and I began arguing. 'Come on then, in the tunnel,' he said.

There were a few heated words, but there was no tunnel meeting. I like Bailey and there were no problems when he joined Millwall. He's a street kid who does whatever he thinks he has to do for his team to win and I respect that.

Instead of heading to the tunnel at the end of the game, I went with the other Millwall players to thank our loyal travelling fans for their support on what is one of the longest journeys they can make.

Win, lose or draw it is important to acknowledge the part played by those who follow Millwall away from home. It is not cheap to travel up and down the country and buy match tickets. Midweek games can often mean driving back to London, returning at maybe three in the morning with work a few hours later.

I have so much admiration for these fans.

✱　✱　✱　✱　✱

ANOTHER ENCOUNTER came in 2013/14 with Karleigh Osborne, who went on to join Bristol City, and maybe I took things too far, but when I train I do so with the same intensity as if it was a league game.

I train as I play which can mean an aggressive edge at times – I am obsessed with playing football and winning, which includes every tackle in training.

I admit my emotions can sometimes get the better of me and I say things I later regret, but we are who we are. There was some ill feeling brewing between us after we each blamed the other for mistakes. I have this bomb inside my head that can occasionally explode. I controlled it better as I became older, but the detonator can still be pressed.

We had a less-than-complimentary conversation and as Osborne came towards me in an aggressive manner I instinctively jabbed him in the mouth as I thought he was going to hit me. There was a bit of a scuffle which was quickly broken up by the other players.

It took a long time to calm Osborne down, his mood not entirely helped by his bleeding lip.

Like most training ground bust-ups, the heat of the moment can sometimes take over, but with a shake of hands and an apology the incident is usually forgotten.

The same season, before the game away to Queens Park Rangers, Steve Mildenhall thought it would be fun to slap tickets I had just sorted out to put into envelopes on to the floor. On other days I may have found it amusing, too, but it was 28 September, the anniversary of my mum's passing, so my emotions were a little raw.

I booted Mildenhall even though he was 6ft 4in. I think he realised he had done the wrong thing at the wrong time and thankfully he did not react because it would have kicked off. Mildenhall, unaware of the circumstances at the time, apologised the following day.

In 2010, a training collision with my still good mate Gary Alexander cost me my place in the League 1 Play-Off Final against Swindon Town at Wembley. I had been sidelined for a month with a foot injury and had returned to training only the day before the incident which gave me ten days to reach full fitness.

I was trying to impress and ran past Alexander who I believed could not get the ball so he tripped me, which at the time I thought was intentional. As he made contact I felt the foot go again and I immediately knew I would be out for another month. I'd been suffering from severe bone bruising, an injury that can take months to heal.

I jumped up, pushed him in the face and grabbed him round the neck, but did not punch him. Alexander said he was sorry and he could see how angry I was, though I felt bad for losing my temper. My reaction was an instinctive panic, fearing the worst.

Aimee once advised me to attend anger management classes in an effort to control my outbursts.

Willie Donachie, one of the most calm and mild-mannered people I have met, once recommended a woman who might be able to help me. The sessions with her were positive and she probed deep into my upbringing to find out why I would suddenly react in the way I did.

Donachie also recommended yoga which Aimee thought was hilarious.

My anger is sometimes triggered by people underestimating me, belittling me or telling me bare-faced lies. I would rather someone tell me how it is, good or bad, and let me make up my mind from there.

With age comes maturity, but I think I will always have an over-aggressive streak in me, though over the years I have learned to control this and use it in a way that will benefit me, particularly on the pitch.

It also took me a long time to realise that for many years my dad was right to warn me about the company I was keeping.

6

My dodgy 'Arsenal' muffins business at school

The headmaster thought it was the crime of the century

AT SCHOOL, like some I experienced bullying and was teased because of my teeth. My parents couldn't afford a proper blazer for me so I had a jacket with the badge sewn on.

I suffered the embarrassment of having a book stamped because I had to have free dinners.

Some say your school days are the best days of your life. I'm not so sure. Unless it was football then me and school never really got on.

The other schoolkids and my street mates told me I had no chance of realising my dream of becoming a professional footballer. All this only drove me to be more successful and prove them wrong.

Growing up on council estates in London wasn't easy, but I feel I'm a tougher and stronger person for it today.

School was no different. In September 1993, I started secondary school at St Aloysius College, Highgate. I had no real interest in school. I was convinced I'd be a footballer one day. My mum and dad weren't as sure as I was and used to nag me about my grades and homework.

I wasn't the most popular at school. I was mocked about my teeth which, because of a skateboard accident when I was younger, meant some were chipped, others were bent and 'buck teeth' used to get a lot of stick.

I used to have free school dinners because my parents weren't earning much money.

It was a total embarrassment standing in the canteen waiting to have my blue book stamped.

Other kids would come in with £2 a day and have a choice of what they could eat or drink.

To improve my financial situation, I started to nick chocolate and blueberry muffins from lorries parked outside Arsenal's old Highbury stadium at night and sell them at school for 50p each, or three for £1 – a lot of money for a young boy to be making.

It wasn't long before someone tried to take a muffin without paying and we ended up fighting in the playground in front of everyone. My takings went everywhere and my younger brother, Gary, tried to pick up as much as he could while others were scrambling for the 50p pieces and £1 coins.

This dubious business went on for about a month before I was eventually rumbled. The headmaster telephoned dad and told him he needed to see him about 'something serious'.

Dad drove straight to school in a panic, while I sat nervously waiting for the verdict. When dad came out of the headmaster's office I thought that was the end of me, but he just said the teacher was so pleased with himself, like he had just solved the crime of the century.

Thankfully dad wasn't as angry as I thought he would be. He told me he was not happy with me nicking stuff and made me promise I would never steal again. I still managed to keep my earnings of around £120 from my little business venture. I splashed out on a Nike puffer jacket from JD Sports.

It was the bollocks, bright yellow.

ONE OF the main reasons I went to St Aloysius College was because it was known to attract the best young football prospects from north London. This also meant I was eligible to play in not only one of the best district sides in London – Islington and Camden – but also in the country.

We had the likes of Joe Cole, who was on West Ham's books, Jay Bothroyd and John Halls, who were at Arsenal, plus Johnnie Jackson of Tottenham, although of all the young prospects in the team, only these four and myself made it all the way to pro level.

Our Islington and Camden team dominated district football for around five years, winning virtually everything. We lost only a couple of games in that period, one against Sefton, a team from Liverpool who we played in a two-legged final.

The first leg was at Goodison Park which we won 2-1, but we lost the return leg at Highbury 3-1. It was while I was playing district football that I was scouted by Mark Curtis who was working for Millwall.

Playing for our district we always wore an Arsenal kit as our coaches were connected to the club.

This was the only occasion I had worn any shirt other than Millwall's.

I was obsessed with football. Apart from sleeping and eating, there was little else I wanted to do. In the council estate where we lived there was a football cage where we would play other local kids. The games weren't five- or six-a-side, the total depended on how many turned up. The goals were painted lines on a brick wall while the surface was gravel, but for us it was all we needed.

There were some Turkish boys from down the road who spoke little English, not that it mattered. Fuck me, they were rough, tough kids though these games never kicked off into fights or anything. It was probably the nearest I'll ever get to international football.

Sun, rain, snow, gales…the weather was irrelevant. Every single day I played football when I came home from school. I soon gained a reputation for being the best street footballer in the area though the most important kid was whoever owned the football. We would knock at his door and ask if he wanted to come out to play, most of the time only because he had the ball.

Crap player, great ball.

There were two kids who lived only doors away, Johnny Mullins, who had a decent career with Rotherham, and John Mackie, who spent eight years with Reading and Leyton

Orient. Not many streets can have produced three professional footballers.

One year there was a schools cup final for St Aloysius at Highbury and as usual my pre-match preparation was a game of cage football. I was late for dinner so I ran home and in sprinting down some steps I twisted an ankle. I limped indoors and my dad put a bandage and Deep Heat on it. Of course, these days it is common knowledge you put ice on a twisted ankle but at the time it used to be Deep Heat 'and you'll be fine'.

When I woke up the next morning I was far from fine.

I couldn't walk though I tried to convince myself I'd be okay. Of course, I was wrong and had to tell the teacher I had hurt an ankle and was unable to play. I was gutted.

Luckily, I had played at Highbury before so I wasn't missing out on a once in a lifetime opportunity.

In fact, going to watch Arsenal convinced me that I had to be a footballer, not that any other profession was ever really in my thoughts.

The first game I attended before joining Millwall was Arsenal v Tottenham. My dad had paid for me to be a Junior Gunner and as much as watching the match, I loved seeing how the players warmed up.

Lee Dixon was always first to appear, then Kevin Campbell, David Rocastle and Perry Groves with Ian Wright and Paul Merson coming out together. To see them knock inch-perfect 60-yard passes to each other was an education and left me open-mouthed in admiration.

My brothers, Gary and Paul, were also good footballers. Gary was on West Ham's books and was spoken of as the next Joe Cole. While Gary had ability, he never possessed the absolute desire or the mental strength to cope with the pressures of high-level football.

The three of us would play football together and there was no brotherly love in our tackles or challenges to the extent it was not unusual to see a family at war with punches exchanged. It was all part of growing up, just as there was one boy in every street who could kick the ball harder than anyone else.

Our cannonball kid was a ginger-haired lad called Aiden and I hated him because he had a shot that was unstoppable. He couldn't do anything else, but jeez could he shoot. For two years I tried to beat him at an end-to-end shooting game but failed.

Playing for my school I was initially a striker and used to score five or six goals each game, but when I reached county level aged nine the standard was much higher. The only way I could get in the team was as a right-back because the front players were so good. I owe John Spooner, our coach, a big debt for this. The team were so successful that I stayed right-back and the rest is history.

I recently read Matthew Syed's fascinating book *Bounce* in which he says it is not so much natural talent but sheer hard work and hours of practice that can take you to the top. Tiger Woods was given a golf club at the age of two and by the time he was eight he was so far ahead of kids older than him. People assumed he had been born with a God-given talent for golf, but it was more because from an early age he was drilled by his father to play golf.

I went on to play for Senrab FC, a Sunday League team based in Wanstead, east London. The list of boys who played for Senrab reads like a who's who – John Terry, Sol Campbell,

Lee Bowyer, Vince Hilaire, Terry Hurlock, Alan Curbishley, Jermain Defoe and Ray Wilkins to name but a few.

So why did I choose Millwall?

I knew the fans had a reputation of being feared and tough which I liked. I was ten years old and being born in August made me a Leo, so I was convinced I was already a Lion.

* * * * *

AS A SCHOOLBOY at Millwall I was a skinny kid, one of the smallest players in training and games. My team-mates and opponents were from the streets of south-east London and the matches weren't for the soft, shy type. You had to hold your own and I was never one to be intimidated, no matter how big the opposition were.

Other players were older, bigger and stronger than me. Many had fully-grown beards, while I had not even started to shave. But I always gave as good as I got and could match anyone for pace and aggression.

Millwall had a lot of players from council estates where they breed them tough. I don't necessarily mean in a violent way, just standing up for yourself in an effort to earn respect. Being mentally strong was as important as anything, but when you are in your early teens a physical presence can help.

A good example was Cherno Samba, who was younger than me and went on to play four times for Gambia's national team. He was a wonder kid from Peckham at 13, but everyone was convinced he was older because of his size.

He may have been in his first year as a teenager, but Samba was built like a brick outhouse and scored 132 goals in 32 games for his boys' club before joining Millwall in 2002.

Samba was everything you wanted from a centre-forward – big, strong and powerful, able to outmuscle even the toughest defenders. He was even tipped to spearhead England's 2006 World Cup attack.

In your early teens size can certainly be a factor because the bigger and stronger you are counts for a lot. By the time Samba was 16 others had caught up with him physically and that is when ability starts to show through with earlier advantages becoming less of a factor.

Samba was the biggest of Millwall's African lads who seemed more naturally powerful than others, but at the same time they were just kids off the street like me and I was hardly Rambo. Training and playing with and against such players taught me never to be intimidated because if anyone showed any weakness they would have never reached stage two of their career.

Millwall released Samba who joined Cadiz in Spain, returning to England with Plymouth (where Ian Holloway was manager) and the last I heard of him he was playing for Tonsberg in the Norwegian Second Division. How the once mighty…

But I think the coaches saw some fight, some animal spirit in this street kid called Alan Dunne.

It was a tough, demanding introduction to football at that level, especially as I was far from being one of the biggest boys at the time, but they were great battles and challenges for me. Most of these kids developed early and when the rest of the lads caught up in size, their ability was less noticeable. By the time they were 15 or 16 most never progressed much further.

We had coaches such as Tom Walley and Kevin O'Cal-laghan, the ex-Millwall and Ipswich winger. They demanded everything and more from their youth teams and Millwall traditionally had one of the best sides in the South East Counties League. This was a league for the youth teams of southern England and while the bigger London clubs tended to dominate, Millwall usually did well and even won it in 1968/69.

However, I had a bigger problem to overcome than opponents.

7

Booted out of home by my dad

But he saved my career

I WAS ALWAYS attracted to the wrong type of company, whether it was at school or on the estate. Trouble was like a magnet for me. Maybe it was because I loved banter and these clowns were always the funny ones.

It became so bad that there were constant rows with dad, to the extent he told me to pack my bags and leave as I refused to listen to his advice about those I was hanging around with.

There were lot of gangs in our area and by the time I was 15, football was not the priority on the estate because it was the era of drugs, stealing, chasing girls and being a nuisance to society.

I couldn't see that these people were bad for me, but dad could. He was right, even though it took me so long to realise it, with many arguments and fights. But he was right all along.

The boys I had played football with growing up were becoming violent and being locked up for various crimes.

'You are who you associate with,' dad used to say to me. How true.

He told me, 'If you carry on going behind my back and socialise with these people you will eventually end up in jail.'

I had to get out of this environment otherwise my football career would probably have ended before it had even started. Dad made the wise decision to phone Bob Pearson, the youth development officer, to see if there was anywhere I could go to find an alternative to the company I was keeping.

Bob spoke to the chairman, Theo Paphitis, who was aware that a possible future asset was becoming a liability. The club found me somewhere to stay, with Gerry Docherty, the Millwall physio, and his wife Deirdre and two kids.

Gerry was a hard, Scottish old school sort of guy who took no nonsense from anyone and commanded huge respect at the club.

I wasn't exactly looking forward to moving in with a mad Scot who had a massive reputation for being strict.

But I had to get away from Highbury if I was to stand any chance of becoming a professional. Gerry and I clicked immediately and I was more than well looked after in every way, especially food – they loved their food. I was the best fed boy, no other player in digs ate like I did.

I spent three years with Gerry, who gave me lots of important advice. He was heavily involved with the first-team staff and would tell me what was needed, what the manager wanted to see and how to behave and conduct myself.

He kept me on the straight and narrow.

As much as anything, he kept me away from the dark distractions of north London. When I look back, dad made the right choice, even if I was far from happy about being shown the door from my family home. Dad could see things I couldn't, or maybe I didn't want to see, and the time I spent with Gerry and Deidre helped me considerably on my journey to eventually becoming pro.

Mind you, there was the occasional run-in, which I can laugh about now (Aimee – please skip the next few paragraphs). One night, I think it was my 18th birthday, I asked Gerry, who was going to be away with the first team, if I could bring back a girl who I was seeing. He said I could and he would let Deidre know.

Happy days, I thought.

The next morning I received a call from Gerry saying he was going to kill me and that Deidre hadn't slept all night because of the laughing, joking and…

I had no reason to disbelieve Gerry from the tone of his voice.

The misunderstanding was that in Gerry's mind, saying 'yes' meant bringing a girl round for the evening, not an all-nighter. It all kicked off the next day when Gerry returned and at 18 I knew it was time to move on.

But before that, Greece was the word for my first boys' holiday.

8

To Greece with no passport

But it was the best boys' holiday ever

I WAS INVITED to go to Kavos on the Greek island of Corfu for two weeks with some of the older lads, Joe Dolan, Steven Reid, Richard Sadlier, Robbie Ryan and my best mate at the time, Mark Hicks. What happens in Kavos…

My first mistake was to put my passport into my suitcase after it had been inspected at check-in. I had no idea I would need it again at passport control so I thought I'd put it in my case for safe-keeping just before they put my baggage through.

It was my first holiday apart from one with my parents when I was young. Somehow I managed to get through two passport controls without a passport, which would be practically impossible in this day and age.

I realised my error and told the authorities, but the bags had already been loaded on the plane. I was advised I had to go to the cargo hold with security to pinpoint which suitcase was mine.

Forty-five minutes later there was still no sign of my bag.

There were cases being moved everywhere in an effort to locate mine. Eventually the pilot requested we take off and I should resume the search for my bag when we landed in Greece.

Unsurprisingly, the passengers were not pleased with the delay which was obvious from the looks I received when I belatedly boarded the plane. No eye contact as I walked guiltily down the aisle.

The lads thought it was hilarious, but I was rightly the target for some serious piss-taking throughout the flight.

Arriving in Greece and going through passport – or in my case, no passport – control – was the easy bit. The airport was packed with young holidaymakers ready to party. Instead of waiting for security to escort me I saw that the Greek authorities weren't even looking at passports. They just waved people through and I saw my opportunity to sneak by without being checked.

Genius, who needs a passport?

MY NEXT lesson in Greek holiday-making was to discover how painful the sun can be. Did I pack sun cream? No. Did I use any? No.

Surprise, surprise, after two days I was burnt to a cinder.

If that was not bad enough, after three days I had spent all my money – £500 – with a week and a half to go.

So much for the two-for-one rubbish.

Dad had to wire me some more money which lasted me a few days, but from then, credit (no pun intended) to the other boys, they looked after me by paying for my dinner and drinks.

The funniest part of the trip involved Mark Hicks who had grown up in the hard streets of Belfast. Hicks and I decided to hire mopeds as we heard you didn't need a full driving licence, only a provisional.

I asked Hicks if he could drive a moped and he replied in his deep Irish accent, 'Aye, of course, I drive them all the time back home.'

Within seconds of driving off, his moped was ten feet in the air.

He had wobbled, panicked, and managed to flip the bike over which landed on top of him. His toes were almost hanging off with his hands and face grazed from the impact.

I said, 'Mate, you're fucked, you need to go to hospital.'

He replied, 'What's the bike like?'

'Fuck the bike,' I said. 'Let's get you to hospital.'

The bike was in a bad way, and so was Hicks. We somehow wheeled the bike back and the look on the owner's face was priceless.

Understandable as we'd only taken the bikes out a few minutes earlier.

Hicks went to hospital to have his toes treated and had a hefty bill waiting for him upon his return to the moped hire shop.

Despite all this, or even because of it, we had the best two weeks a group of young lads could have and I will never forget the laughs we shared.

* * * * *

I DID NOT learn from my Greek passport malfunction because when I went on another lads' holiday to Ayia Napa a few years later I had not realised my passport was out of date.

It had expired two weeks previously and officials at Heathrow Airport had to obtain clearance from their counterparts in Cyprus to enable me to fly to Larnaca.

Thankfully, permission was granted by Cyprus, but I spent a lot of time on holiday going to various government offices to ensure I would be able to return to England.

9

I was not living the lifestyle of a professional

Two years of my career were wasted

I MOVED ON from Gerry and Deirdre Docherty and not for the first time I fell into bad company. I moved in with a 28-year-old girl, ten years my elder, who lived in east London. I was arguing with dad again, unable to go home, so it was convenient for me to share her council house.

This was another poor decision and something I regret.

I was in the reserves at the time and Mark McGhee would give us Saturday and Sunday off. I trained or played Monday to Friday so effectively had a two-and-a-half-day weekend.

I was earning £750 a week and had just a phone and a car to pay for. I had no major outgoings, yet I was doing nothing productive with my time or money and once again

I was surrounded by the wrong type of people while staying there.

I wasn't living the lifestyle my job demanded and I felt lost.

I wasted two, maybe two and a half years of my career which I can never get back. I needed someone who could help me turn my life around though I had no idea I would meet her at Delano's nightclub in Bromley, one of my regular haunts. One night during the off-season I went there with someone who was, you won't be shocked to learn, not the best influence on me.

I had just come back from a boys' holiday with Mark Phillips in Cancún. That morning I had collected my brand new Mercedes so I asked my pal if he fancied heading over to Bromley in my new set of wheels.

I remember this day like it was yesterday. I had a brand new (to match the car) white Prada top, a Merc straight from the showroom and a Mexican Desperate Dan.

It was obvious to me some girl was going to get lucky. Little did I know it would be the girl I was to marry.

When I saw her I thought how stunning she was and my opinion has never changed, though to this day I am adamant that it was Aimee who spoke to me first.

Aimee's comeback story, which I'll never live down, concerns her shoes. After a day at Ascot she was complaining that her feet were tired. She says I kept asking her if she wanted to leave her shoes in my car – my concerns were not so much her feet and as cringeworthy as it sounds now, I just wanted to show off my new car. Maybe even get a sneaky kiss.

She loves telling the story as much as I hate hearing it. I can't believe what a flash bastard I was trying to be but hey, you're only young once.

My reply to all this is, 'Well, I did something right…12 years later we're still together.'

We immediately hit it off. Aimee was a young girl from west London working in a bank at Canary Wharf who had bought her own flat, completed a business degree from Bath University and achieved A grades in all of her A levels.

What did she see in me? They say opposites attract.

I knew straight away that Aimee was not just another girl and things quickly became quite serious. Like me, Aimee had lost her mum at a young age and in similar circumstances tragedies like these can often bring people together.

Aimee taught me the social graces that had passed me by. I had no idea what a glass of red wine was or what to ask for in a decent restaurant.

The standard order for the Dunne family had been a well done steak and chips, washed down with a pint of Coke.

Aimee opened my eyes to a new life and a new lifestyle. Six months after meeting her I had bought my own flat and six months after that she had moved in with me. Kevin Braniff, a team-mate who was living with me at the time, wasn't too happy when I told him he had to leave.

But it was no great surprise.

THE 2005/06 season proved to be Gerry Docherty's last at The Den. He was sacked by Millwall on 1 February 2006, following a falling-out with striker Barry Hayles who was injured and should have been walking with the aid of crutches.

We were having a team meal at a hotel in London, paid for by the new chairman, Peter de Savary. Gerry, along with the players, had enjoyed a drink or two. When he saw Hayles walking without his crutches, his dark mood was not helped by Jody Morris teasing Gerry on the karaoke mic.

Gerry snapped and headed straight for Hayles. He shouted, 'Are you taking the piss out of me?'

The pair almost came to blows with me having to keep them apart. Colin Lee was the manager and he sacked Gerry that night. Gerry took the club to a court of arbitration where things became very messy with a lot of mud hitting the fan. I was asked to speak on Gerry's behalf, effectively to defend him and testify against Hayles.

It was a no-win situation for me; whatever I did I would upset someone, so I pleaded the fifth and said nothing. Gerry and Deirdre were very upset, believing that after all they had done for me I should have helped them. On the other hand, to go against a team-mate, and by extension the manager, would not have worked in my favour.

I didn't agree with what Hayles had done, at the same time Gerry did not handle the situation very well. If what I did, or perhaps did not do, sounds selfish, I felt I had to look after myself and I don't regret my decision.

Since then I've had virtually no contact with Gerry and it was a sour way to end what had been a lovely three years with him and his family.

10

Blood, sweat and no fears

Some players cannot handle playing for Millwall

THEY WERE the same two questions each time a player joined Millwall. 'What's it like to play for Millwall? Are the fans really that bad?'

My answer was, 'It is wonderful to play for Millwall and no, the fans are that GOOD. Show them you love the club and once they are on your side they will be the best supporters in the world.'

Millwall fans demand a level of pride in the shirt and passion from players that matches their own love for the club. They will accept a player not being over-skilful, but he must…MUST…show that he wants to wear the Millwall jersey, that he will bust a gut for the club and is honoured to be a Lion.

This is not something that can be coached, it is either inside you or it is not and can make playing for Millwall difficult for some players if they do not have that special fire in their belly.

The Millwall manager, whoever he may be, knows this is a major factor when it comes to scouting players.

He looks a good player, but is he a Millwall player? Could he cope with the demands of playing for Millwall?

I've seen some players shaking with fear before their debuts at The Den and they are from the home team. They are obviously not ready, worried by the reputation of Millwall supporters before they know what they are really like.

When your mindset is, 'If I make a mistake they'll be at me,' you have no chance of becoming a Lion.

The attitude must be, 'If I make a mistake, fuck it. Whatever the error, I will come out on top.' There has to be a confidence and arrogance that you can overcome any early adversity.

When I was a YTS I was taught how to deal with what it means to play for Millwall. We were almost broken and rebuilt as people, which was a massive part of gaining an inner strength…to never, ever give up.

I don't think it happens these days, but it certainly helped players such as Paul Robinson and I as we came through the ranks.

Many a game I have played in, especially at The Den, if the ball is there to be won, then it has to be won. Under no circumstances must you pull out. No second thoughts. No other options. You have to go in full steam.

Millwall fans love ball players, but as much as anything they appreciate ball winners, those who give their absolute all in terms of work ethic, those who chase lost causes, those who constantly harass opponents and end every game with their shirt drenched with the sweat of someone who could not have given any more for the cause.

This is the Millwall way.

It is an inner spirit, a drive, a passion. It isn't just going around kicking people, simply possessing a hunger to succeed that the diehard Millwall supporters will love.

Once they are on your side there is no better feeling and on occasions when I gave my all but was sent off it was almost as if I had scored a goal, given the support from the thousands of Millwall fans.

* * * * *

NEIL HARRIS is rightly a Millwall legend. Up there with the all-time greats of the club. His 125 league goals make him Millwall's record scorer, beating Teddy Sheringham's total of 111. Yet perhaps surprisingly Harris was chosen as the Player of the Year only once, in 1999, his first year with the club during his two spells at The Den totalling ten years. This shouldn't be seen as a slight against him, it merely underlines that sometimes the supporters look for other qualities when the award comes round.

Blood and sweat, but no fears.

Since Steve Claridge lifted the award in 2003, every subsequent winner has been either a defender or a defensive player: Tony Warner, Darren Ward (twice), David Livermore, Richard Shaw, Paul Robinson, Andy Frampton, myself, Tamika Mkandawire, Jimmy Abdou (twice), Danny Shittu and David Forde.

No coincidence. These are the type of players Millwall fans salute.

Going back further, players such as Barry Kitchener and Keith Stevens typified what Millwall are all about, true Lions who the supporters knew would never let them down. It is unrealistic to expect every player to have the spirit of Kitch and Rhino, but at Millwall you need a balance including what the legends of the club gave to achieve consistent results.

What I learned in my 23 years at The Den was that as soon as you cross the line of acceptance with Millwall fans they will support you, whatever happens. Some players never manage it and it took me some time to appreciate what gets the crowd passionate and excited. I needed to work out a formula whereby I could please the fans yet still play my own game.

For the early part of my career I did not have that rapport with the supporters. I was booed and constantly criticised on the Millwall fan forums.

I remember a fan walking past me after a game and asking, 'When are you going to fuck off out of this club?'

I was tempted to follow him and rip his head off, but players should not react, though it is not always easy to remain silent.

'Come here and say that to my face,' I replied. He carried on walking. Had he turned back I hate to think what I would have done.

It became worse the year after we were relegated to League 1 in 2006 when many players left and escaped the anger of the rightly frustrated fans.

If I gave the ball away I could hear the crowd moaning and groaning. I had no real relationship with them and there was one section that seemed to be on my back no matter what I did, ready to criticise my first mistake. Every club has a scapegoat and for a while I felt I was Millwall's, especially when we lost. My body language probably underlined there was little chemistry between me and the supporters, but it was something I learned how to fix over the years.

Yes, I had the option to leave. Did I run and jump ship like some because we were relegated? No, and with no regrets.

I had always been happy at Millwall and while I could possibly have earned a few more quid by going elsewhere, I made the right decision to stay.

I had options to leave the club earlier, even abroad to clubs such as Hapoel Tel Aviv and the New England Revolution of Major League Soccer.

When the chance to go to Tel Aviv came up, I was in the last year of my contract and the club were bringing in one right-back after another. I had to re-assess my situation and it did cross my mind that a change might help. There was the added incentive of Champions League football plus an improved salary, a free car and accommodation.

Aimee was not keen on going to Israel because of the civil unrest in the country and the transfer was a non-starter.

Moving to Boston did not involve the problems of Tel Aviv, and Steve Nicol, coach of the Revolution, spoke with my then agent, Johnny Mac. It would have been a step down in terms of the quality of football I was used to and it never progressed any further than a chat with Mac.

I made the right decision by sticking with the club and tried to win the fans over. I did not take the easy option to give up. This was not in my DNA. I never quit. I go again and again until I get there.

I came through what was the toughest part of my career. Slowly things improved and eventually the fans voted me the Player of the Year while I also scored the Goal of the Season at Walsall as we returned to the Championship in 2010.

These are awards I will always cherish and keep on my mantelpiece.

* * * * *

MILLWALL ARE a working-class, blue-collar club set in the heartland of south-east London. While most other areas of London have undergone extensive redevelopment, the south-east seemed to be the last to be upgraded. A trip down the Old Kent Road, the Walworth Road or around Deptford shows there is still much to be done, but it is from such places that many of Millwall's most loyal fans come.

They are what I call real people who work hard for their money to support Millwall.

Maybe some supporters expect too much too soon, especially from new signings, but players have to work out a way to show the fans how good they really are.

Kevin Braniff remains a close pal and he went through a spell when he was booed, even if he was on the bench. When George Friend spent a month on loan to Millwall from Wolves in 2009 he could not understand why one fan called him the c-word ten minutes into his debut. Attempting a pass down the channel, Friend had put the ball into the stand on two occasions.

Friend was such a nice kid but he was not cut out for Millwall because he never came back from this. He didn't even want to play the second half.

In January 2013 Rob Hulse joined Millwall on loan from Queens Park Rangers for the remainder of the season. Hulse played 11 games for us, his last against Blackburn when he scored an own goal in our 2-1 Championship defeat.

The crowd got on his back and not only did Hulse have no wish to play for Millwall again, within a few months I heard he had retired to move into physiotherapy.

A problem can be that if one fan boos a player, others will follow, but that is part of football. If a player shows the wrong body language or is not seen to be giving what he should then supporters will not be slow in showing their frustration.

On the other hand, there are players who have joined Millwall and immediately become local heroes. Nicky Bailey signed from Middlesbrough in 2003 and while he had been booed when he played at The Den for Charlton, he hit the ground running as a Lion.

I think Bailey was jeered because he was such a good player for our south-east London neighbours. When he joined Millwall the fans loved him straight away as he steamed into tackles with the desire demanded.

✳   ✳   ✳   ✳   ✳

AS A schoolboy I used to take the train and then walk from South Bermondsey station to The Den and this gave me a real feeling, a true understanding of Millwall. I would stroll past the pubs – all have traditional English names, none of your fancy Primrose and Pancake or whatever – proudly wearing my Millwall tracksuit.

I could sense the passion, dedication, feeling and intensity of the Millwall supporters.

On my journey home to north London, my Millwall tracksuit was almost like a badge of honour. On occasions I would be among hundreds, even thousands of Arsenal fans as they made their way from Highbury, yet not one ever said a word to me. Wearing my club tracksuit made me feel big, important, and of course proud. Whether it gave out the impression that I should be respected or even a fear factor I don't know, but rightly or wrongly it is something I loved being associated with.

However, being the Millwall player who has been shown the most number of red cards is another matter.

11

Millwall's most sent-off player

I do not think I am a dirty player

I AM the most sent-off player in Millwall's history. Ten red cards, four straight, six of them second cautionable offences (and one straight red on my second Leyton Orient league start). Seventy-nine yellow cards (and one for Leyton Orient).

Three one-game suspensions for accumulating five cautions by the beginning of December. Twice I incurred a two-match ban for reaching ten cautions by the second Sunday in April (plus a £15 fine).

Banned for 31 games, the equivalent of more than half a season, and around £30,000 worse off because of it.

These are not statistics I am proud of, yet at the same time I don't have a feeling of deep shame. Only three, maybe four, of my dismissals were, in my view, justified. One taught me a lot about the internal workings of the Football Association's disciplinary process.

I don't feel I'm a dirty player, just that I had a passion every Millwall supporter not so much expects, but demands. Each player is different, but if I am being honest to myself, this reflects who I am as a person and a player – plenty of heart and no fear. Always giving everything and more.

This is Millwall as I know it.

There were many good times, but inevitably there were also bad days, off days in the literal sense. Here are my ten red cards and the reasons behind them. I'll let you make up your own mind.

* * * * *

MILLWALL 1 NOTTINGHAM FOREST 0
3 October 2004
Referee: Richard Beeby
Second yellow card, 75 minutes
One-game ban
I had been cautioned three minutes into the second half for a foul on Andy Reid and in the 75th minute I slid in on Alan Rogers. Neither foul was worthy of a yellow card and that was not only my opinion – the view of the match reports the following day was that both cautions were harsh.

I was also brought down inside the penalty area which the press coverage agreed was a stick-on spot-kick, but nothing was given.

Richard Beeby also came in for criticism from Nottingham Forest manager Joe Kinnear who was angry about the free kick from which David Livermore scored the winner.

CARDIFF CITY 0 MILLWALL 1

2 February 2005

Referee: Mike Jones

Straight red card, 90th minute

Six-game ban

This is, without doubt, the worst, most unjust red card of my career.

David Livermore and Cardiff's James Collins were also sent off while manager Dennis Wise was so angry at what he was seeing he threw a bottle of water to the ground – unfortunately it bounced up and struck an assistant referee which led to Wise being sent to the stand. This was typical Wisey, though.

I was playing in midfield and we were leading 1-0 with the clock winding down. To waste time – legitimately – I ran with the ball towards the corner flag. In trying to win possession, Chris Barker clipped me and I fell to the ground.

Barker thought I was play-acting and tried to drag me up. In doing so he pulled my shirt almost over my head, nearly choking me. I pushed him away by putting my hands on his chest and within seconds the already red hot atmosphere of the final moments was turned up a notch with a mass brawl, other players surrounding myself and the referee.

When some sort of peace had been restored, the referee came over and showed me a straight red card. I could not believe it. All I had done was to push, not over-aggressively, an opponent away after he had attempted to pull me up from the ground by my shirt.

Violent conduct? It wasn't even handbags. More like purses.

Maybe the ref thought that as in his eyes I had been the instigator of the trouble, I had to go. I argued my point, but with a deep sense of injustice about the dismissal, a red mist appeared when I left the field of play. Angry and frustrated, I returned to put my case to the referee again which proved to be a big mistake.

A two-game mistake.

When I arrived in the dressing room I was still fuming, my mood not helped when a few seconds later Livermore walked in – another red card victim – while outside it was all still going off with Wise and the water bottle.

Amusing for both sets of fans, no doubt.

The club looked at the video footage of my incident and we decided to appeal for wrongful dismissal on the grounds that what I did was not violent conduct. Along with representatives of the club, I went, suited and booted, to the central London offices of the Professional Footballers' Association where the hearing was held. The PFA was very confident of the red card being overturned because in its view 'there was nothing in it'.

Apparently there was. Quite a lot, in fact.

There were four elderly gentlemen representing the Football Association who would make their decision based on video evidence. I was briefed to apologise to the disciplinary panel which I did – reluctantly – telling them exactly what had happened. I felt confident when they left the room to look at a recording of the incident that my appeal would be upheld, yet when they returned they told me I had lost and worse was to come. They handed me a six-game ban.

As it was my second red card of the season, on the totting-up process it was three matches plus one. Because I did not leave the field of play immediately they added a further two games to the suspension and a hefty fine. A six-game ban for pushing an opponent away after he had dragged me up by my jersey.

I was not guilty of a nasty tackle or planting an elbow in someone's face. I just pushed away an opponent who had acted in an aggressive manner towards me.

The disciplinary commission came to the view that as I did not leave the field of play quickly I was guilty of starting the brawl, hence the extra two games.

Things were going well for me at the time and the victory over Cardiff had been a massive win for us, but the red card took the edge off of what should have been a cause for celebration.

If there was any positive about going almost five weeks without a game, it was that Wise allowed me to take Aimee on a short holiday to Dubai, thus escaping the snow of England.

I was left very disillusioned by the disciplinary process that saw me given a six-game ban. I admit I was wrong to continue to argue my point, but in the heat of the battle and feeling, knowing, I had done little wrong, it was difficult to accept such an injustice and simply walk away.

Perhaps the commission thought they had to punish me for this and could not do so without turning down the wrongful dismissal appeal, but six matches for a non-violent push did not seem anything like a natural sense of justice.

QUEENS PARK RANGERS 1 MILLWALL 0
11 February 2006
Referee: Alan Wiley
Second yellow card, 76th minute
One-game ban
Our spirits were up – of course they were, it was a derby game – but in the 76th minute I was sent off for elbowing Steve Lomas, who seven years later was to be my manager at

Millwall. Then the police got involved as I became a Loftus Road cleaner.

It was some afternoon.

One of my team-mates had told me to wind up Lomas 'because he's been known to react'. The ball came towards us and as we jumped for it I caught Lomas in the face with an elbow. We both hit the deck with Marc Bircham, who later joined Millwall's coaching staff, pinching me under an arm as he 'helped' me to my feet. Of course, I retaliated and a number of Rangers players surrounded me.

I was a shade fortunate it was not a straight red card. I was aware I had been cautioned five minutes earlier, but I thought if I could get away with it how well it would go down with the Millwall fans.

It was an ill-advised challenge, though.

As I walked down the tunnel I took my aggression out on a bin that was full of empty water bottles and stuff, booting it as hard as I could.

I reached the changing room and about 30 seconds later the police and stewards came in to advise me that I should put everything back in the bin.

It was embarrassing, but in order to not attract any more attention and trouble I took their advice, feeling like I was at school again.

The game at Loftus Road was the first in charge for Queens Park Rangers' caretaker manager Gary Waddock, who played for Millwall between 1989 and 1991. Waddock took over from Ian Holloway who had been placed on gardening leave by Rangers. It must be rare that a single incident can effectively involve three managers with Millwall connections past and future.

Lomas did not mention the sending off when he was appointed to succeed Kenny Jackett, he just shook my hand, there were no hard feelings and I had already heard he wasn't the sort of person to hold grudges.

NORTHAMPTON 3 MILLWALL 0
23 January 2007
Referee: Ray Olivier
Straight red card, 90th minute
Three-game ban
Another last-minute dismissal, a pattern was developing. This one was a high, dangerous tackle on Bradley Johnson, who had been giving me verbals throughout the game. I went in studs-up. It was a 50-50 ball, but I caught him.

In these situations you have a split second to ask yourself, 'Is he going to do me, or am I going to do him?'

I thought I'd get away with it, but I didn't.

YEOVIL TOWN 2 MILLWALL 0
10 April 2009
Referee: Andy Hall
Second yellow card, 72nd minute
One-game ban
Millwall had set a club record of six consecutive away wins, but that run was ended by a Yeovil team battling to stay in League 1. Both my yellow cards were for fouls on Tottenham Hotspur's Andros Townsend, on loan to Yeovil, whose Huish Park has seen mixed fortunes for me – I have scored, been sent off and broken a foot there.

The first caution came on 26 minutes and both yellow cards were similar. Townsend was quick, very quick and he pushed the ball past me. In fact, Townsend was so fast that when I went in for the ball it wasn't there. I knew what was coming.

MILLWALL 2 LEICESTER CITY 0
28 December 2010
Referee: Mike Russell

Straight red card, 54th minute

Three-game ban

This was not the best way to celebrate being captain of Millwall for the first time. Leading the team and wearing the armband made me feel powerful and strong, it gave me more adrenalin which at times can give you a rush of blood to the head.

Richie Wellens had been yapping away at me so I went into him with a two-footed tackle. I can have no arguments with the referee's decision, though I am convinced it was Wellens's reaction that made up Mike Russell's mind. As Wellens was rolling around on the floor like he had been shot I was surrounded by Leicester players. The ref had no choice but to show me the red card for serious foul play to try to calm things down.

I didn't think Russell was going to dismiss me initially, but at the same time I have no real defence for this one. Millwall fans clapped me off, which was an unbelievable feeling because even though I had been red-carded they backed me the whole way.

After the game I waited for Wellens in the tunnel, still livid about his reaction which was designed to get me dismissed. Words were exchanged and I was taken away by team-mates to prevent anything further kicking off. Probably just as well.

MILLWALL 3 CARDIFF CITY 3
19 March 2011
Referee: Anthony Taylor
Second yellow card, 90th minute
Two-game ban

A hat-trick of 90th-minute red cards. This was my second sending-off of 2010/11 and involved Craig Bellamy, which probably doesn't come as a huge surprise.

Paul Robinson had gone off injured after 27 minutes and handed me the captain's armband.

Bellamy, who had dominated the game, was one of English football's quickest players and it was a 50-50 ball as he came towards me. If he had got past me he would almost certainly have scored. It was in the 90th minute so it was either stupidity or experience that saw me stop Bellamy going through on goal

I did what I felt I had to do, Millwall fans agreeing because again they clapped me as I walked off.

Mind you, I suspect their mood was dictated by the victim of the tackle as much as the challenge itself.

This was also the game in which a Cardiff fan fell 20 feet from the upper tier of a stand while celebrating the opening goal scored by Chris Burke. He was treated for almost half an hour by the medics before being taken to hospital.

It was a miracle he was not seriously injured as he landed on the seats below. I did not see the incident, I was told by a Cardiff player – ironically Bellamy – during the match.

MILLWALL 0 BIRMINGHAM CITY 6
14 January 2012
Referee: Jon Moss
Straight red card, 57th minute
Three-game ban

I really dislike this lot. Shane Lowry was sent off in the 22nd minute for a foul on Nikola Žigić, but it was only after my dismissal for a challenge on the Serbia international that Birmingham ran riot. Whatever the scoreline, this game was never as one-sided as 6-0 may suggest.

There are some players you think about before games for crunching purposes for no reason other than they irritate you.

Žigić is one of those because he never passes up a chance to win a free kick.

Though Žigić is nearer seven feet tall than six, when the ball landed between us I had my chance and there could only be one winner. The Millwall crowd disliked Žigić and I went in from the side, catching him on the shin. He fell down theatrically, almost in instalments, and the red card was shown to me immediately, which was fair enough.

The three-game ban for serious foul play was not the end of my punishment. I was also fined £2,000 and warned about my future conduct by the Football Association for retweeting a critical comment about referee Jon Moss.

While I could not defend my red card, some Millwall supporters took to Twitter to criticise the referee. On the way home from The Den, I read one tweet which said something to the effect that Millwall 'never get anything from referees' which I retweeted.

Unfortunately, I did not read the tweet through to the end and did not notice '#fuckedupfa'.

In the FA's eyes, a retweet is a form of endorsement for the original sentiments and the following day when I looked at the tweet in its entirety I immediately deleted it.

Too late, the damage had been done.

I received a phone call from Millwall to tell me the FA was investigating my tweet. I was sent a form asking for my observations; why I retweeted it, what my thinking was behind it.

For the record, I was found guilty of breaking FA Rule E3, which dictates that players 'shall at all times act in the best interests of the game and shall not act in any manner which is improper or brings the game into disrepute or use any one, or a combination of, violent conduct, serious foul play, threatening, abusive, indecent or insulting words or behaviour'.

The fact that the comments were not mine was irrelevant and it was the first time I had been charged by the FA, but they felt they had to make an example of me and fined me £2,000.

In fact, the process was the FA fined Millwall and the club deducted the money from my wages.

Kenny Jackett did not say anything to me, personally, about the incident, but he told the press, 'To some degree Alan has been made an example of, but I will vouch for him because Alan Dunne is a very solid and reliable lad who has been unfortunate in these circumstances.

'Twitter is a new thing and sometimes individual opinions can overlap on what is best for the club and what is best for the team, but I'm sure it will all settle down.'

The manager called a meeting where he said there would not be a ban on players using Twitter, but we were all sent a letter warning us about what we say on social networks.

Twitter is here to stay and I believe more clubs are educating players about the world of social media.

Footballers must learn to be careful what they say. Any comments – or even retweets – about referees are likely to land you in trouble.

We have to live with abuse and while it is tempting to reply to someone who has slagged you off, it is best to ignore them or block them.

BRIGHTON 1 MILLWALL 1
31 August 2013
Referee: Robert Madley

Second yellow card, 76th minute

One-game ban

I was cautioned in the 56th minute for time-wasting when we were leading 1-0. There were no ball boys at the Amex so when the ball went into the stand we had to retrieve it ourselves, which took time. The referee kept moaning about how long it was taking, but it couldn't be done any quicker.

Under pressure from the home crowd, the ref initially cautioned me for delaying the restart and 20 minutes later I tackled Andrea Orlandi. It was a nothing foul, maybe a free kick, but inevitably the Brighton supporters were baying for blood and wanted me sent off. Robert Madley obliged. It was only my second foul of the match and the double-whammy was that Brighton equalised with a couple of minutes remaining.

I felt like I had let the team down even though I did not think the dismissal was justified.

BOURNEMOUTH 5 MILLWALL 2
5 October 2013
Referee: Lee Collins
Second yellow card, 58th minute
Two-game ban

Millwall were 2-0 ahead thanks to goals by Martyn Waghorn and Liam Trotter when I was cautioned for a body-check in the 14th minute. We had blown a two-goal lead and it was 3-2 to Bournemouth when, in the 58th minute, I was judged to have handled the ball inside the penalty area – second yellow card, red card, penalty converted, 4-2.

A long throw-in had landed in our penalty area, and because of the sun I was blinded for a split second. The ball bounced, a Bournemouth player kicked it and it struck my hand which was by my side, not at an unnatural angle. It was ball to hand rather than deliberate handball. The ball was kicked so fiercely and from so near it was impossible for me to have reacted.

You cannot appeal a second yellow card – or any yellow card – so there was nothing I could do. As it was my second dismissal of the season I was given a two-game suspension.

Two matches for not being able to get out of the way of a shot from a player who was about a yard from me.

I was very frustrated and in the changing room afterwards Steve Lomas didn't help my mood when he grilled me, blaming me for the result. I stood my ground because I felt I was hard done by and could have done nothing to avoid being hit by the ball.

Other players tend not to interfere when things get heated between the manager and a player, but if team-mates argue others will step in with their own opinion.

This one was strictly me and Lomas.

For whatever reason, Lomas had a different view of the handball when he spoke to the press because he was supportive of me, saying, 'There were some poor decisions from the referee, including the red card to Dunne. How was that a deliberate handball? It's one thing to give a penalty for that incident, but another thing to send him off and it was very harsh.'

Private blame, but public support. Interesting.

* * * * *

THE FOOTBALL ASSOCIATION fines you £10 for a dismissal and £8 for a yellow card.

Millwall usually fined a player only if he had been shown a red card for violent conduct. I think I was only ever fined for the Nikola Žigić dismissal, while my other indiscretions were always suspended fines.

When serving a ban I still received my basic wage but I lost out on appearance money or win bonuses. I estimate this to have cost me around £30,000 in loss of earnings and fines during my 15 bans.

Losing money hurts, but the biggest disappointment was missing games, in my case 30. On four occasions I was suspended for matches against Crystal Palace and watching Millwall play our south-east London rivals from the stand was hugely frustrating.

After my second red card of 2013/14 against Bournemouth I faced the prospect of being fined two weeks' wages for any third dismissal plus two extra games added to the suspension on the totting-up process. This was on my mind for a while and perhaps I subconsciously hesitated when going in for tackles.

It was soon business as usual, though, and I finished the season with four more yellow cards, but no further dismissals.

Ten red cards, but I managed more than double that in goals for Millwall.

12

My favourite five goals

I dedicated my first to my mum

I SCORED 23 goals for Millwall; four winners, four equalisers, four in the last minute, one brace, 13 away, ten at home. Oh, and two penalties which, like buses, came along together.

Millwall lost only three of the 22 games in which I scored. Not exactly in the Neil Harris class, but not bad for a right-back turned central defender.

Choosing my top five goals is no doubt a little easier for me than for Millwall's record scorer, though there was a fair bit of chopping and changing before I settled on my fab five.

No. 1

MY FAVOURITE goal has to be my first for Millwall in the 2-1 win over Gillingham at The Den in October 2004, my 44th-minute strike making it 2-0. It was my first game back after suspension and Jody Morris, who was one of the best passers in the game, slipped me an inch-perfect ball. I ran on to the pass and scored from the edge of the penalty area.

My first reaction was to look to the sky and dedicate the goal to my mum. I blessed myself a couple of times, but my main emotion was with mum.

There can be no better feeling than scoring your first goal for the club you have supported.

It was certainly my most enjoyable goal. Like most kids in the school playground or playing street football, I always used to imagine I was a hero scoring a goal. My idols were not Ian Wright, Paul Gascoigne or Paul Merson like many of my pals. Mine were players who few would have heard of, the likes of Dave Savage, Paul Shaw or Danny Hockton who were Millwall stars at the time.

Scoring fantasy Millwall goals was only a dream, but the real thing was incredible and maybe some kid now thinks he is Alan Dunne as he tucks one away. Well, you never know.

For the record, Barry Hayles had given us the lead with what was also his first goal for Millwall. Modesty forbids me from saying who supplied the pass.

No. 2

RUNNER-UP is the equaliser at Walsall in March 2010 – we were 2-1 down in the third minute of stoppage time. When the ball was headed clear by a Walsall defender it landed just on the edge of the box. On the half-volley I smashed it left-footed into the top corner of the net from 25 yards. Quite a few goals came with my left foot, something which I have worked hard in training to improve.

Millwall fans voted it the Goal of the Season, but for me it meant we had won a crucial point which helped us to reach the play-offs, beating Swindon in the final at Wembley. It was, by far, the best goal I have scored, though nothing can match the pride of opening my Millwall account against Gillingham.

No. 3

ANOTHER last-minute goal, a header that gave Millwall a 3-2 victory at Rotherham in September 2006. We were 2-0 down at one stage but pulled level thanks to two goals by Danny Haynes, his second in the 86th minute with me providing the assist for the equaliser.

With the seconds ticking away Chris Hackett beat his full-back, drove to the line and whipped in a high ball from the right. Knowing the sort of cross Hackett would put over, I read it and timed my run perfectly to outjump a defender on the far post to head home.

Willie Donachie was the manager and he was under pressure as we were struggling at the time. I liked Donachie and I ran over to him to celebrate, to show togetherness and that the team was with him.

No. 4

MY SPECIALITY for late goals continued away to Leicester City in March 2013, the only goal of the match. I had always wanted to score against Kasper Schmeichel, a very good goalkeeper who inherited a lot of his dad's arrogance that almost made you think you could not beat him.

To score the winner in any game is huge, but to do it against a keeper of Schmeichel's ability and a club with the pedigree of Leicester was even more satisfying. The bonus was that the match was televised live by Sky Sports.

In the 87th minute Richard Chaplow cut the ball back to me and I beat Schmeichel with a right-footed shot from just inside the penalty area. I ran to our travelling fans to celebrate a big goal for the club, almost being sent off in the process.

I was about to take off my shirt – it was halfway over my head – when I suddenly remembered I had already been booked. Luckily I kept the shirt on and stayed on the pitch.

One of my close pals, Tommy Pratt, had never seen me score. Unfortunately for Tommy, who was watching the game on TV at home, when I netted my first goal since August 2010 he was in the toilet. His son Caley called out, 'Dad, Dunney's scored.'

As Tommy pulled up his trousers he yelled, 'Are you fucking kidding me? I've waited three years for Dunney to score.'

Mother Nature 1, Dunney's Goal 0.

No. 5

LAST, but by no means least, is my goal against Birmingham City in the Carling Cup at The Den in November 2005. It was in the 57th minute and from a throw-in I held off a challenge from Walter Pandiani before beating Nico Vaesen with a rising left-footed shot to make it 1-1.

That was the score after 90 minutes and with both sides scoring in extra time, penalties were needed to decide the winners. I converted my kick, but Birmingham won the shoot-out 4-3 after Hayles and Ben May missed for Millwall.

❋   ❋   ❋   ❋   ❋

THEY WERE my five best goals while my first 'real' penalty was in November 2007 in the 2-2 draw against Swansea City. Kenny Jackett was in the stands before officially taking over the next day. In the 70th minute Kevin Austin handled the ball and as I wanted to get off to a good start with the new manager I picked up the ball and placed it on the spot. We had no designated penalty taker, just whoever felt confident at the time.

I was also going through a bad spell with the fans and with the score 1-1 I was happy to take the responsibility. I scored, the ball going into the roof of the net, but Paul Anderson made it 2-2 eight minutes later against Jackett's old club.

Four days later, in an FA Cup tie away to Altrincham – Jackett's first match in charge – I scored my second penalty after Chris Lane had handled Gary Alexander's shot, which saw him sent off. That made it 1-1 with Will Hoskins, on loan from Watford, later scoring the winner.

In August 2009, Millwall's League 1 season opener away to Southampton was live on Sky Sports. Matthew Paterson gave Saints' new manager Alan Pardew a good start by opening the scoring in the 51st minute. On 64 minutes we were awarded a penalty when Jason Price was bundled over by Wayne Thomas, but Kelvin Davis saved my kick. Thankfully, a header by Jimmy Abdou, yes Jimmy Abdou – a collector's item, that – a couple of minutes later earned Millwall a point.

However, there is one goal that remains closest to my heart.

13

The brave soldiers made defeat by Brentford so memorable

I was proud leading the team out in our camouflage kit

THE MOST SPECIAL goal I have scored was in the 3-2 defeat by Brentford at The Den on 8 November 2014. I made the score 2-2 before Danny Shittu's own goal gave Brentford victory but despite our defeat, it was the day and the occasion that made everything unforgettable.

We wore a special one-off camouflage colours kit on the day before Remembrance Sunday to commemorate the 100th anniversary of the start of the First World War. Ten pounds from the sale of each replica kit went to Headley Court Army

Rehabilitation Centre. To lead out the team wearing a unique shirt made me very proud. It was a wonderful gesture by the club to help the wounded soldiers who I met as part of the build-up.

Hearing their stories and what they had been through was a real eye-opener so to be captain against Brentford on Memorial Weekend is something I shall never forget.

Yet the story had a far from upbeat beginning.

*   *   *   *   *

AS MILLWALL captain I was asked, along with three other players, if I would go to Headley Court, near Leatherhead in Surrey on a Thursday afternoon to do 'something with the Army'. Everything was top secret and at that time we had no idea about the one-off special kit.

We were travelling to an away game the following day and I was far from pleased about the disruption to the usual match build-up. Lee Martin, Scott McDonald and Ángel Martínez joined me in this magical mystery tour, all of us moaning about having to sample the delights of the M25 when we could be resting. How wrong we were to whinge about what we were about to experience.

We were greeted by some Army top brass along with Deano Standing, Millwall's media and PR consultant, and Lucy Pepper, the media and PR manager. I was taken into the officers' mess – which was anything but a mess – where it was explained that Millwall were to wear a special camouflage kit with a poppy on it for the Brentford game.

I began to appreciate why details of the trip had been kept secret as news of the kit would be announced in the next couple of weeks. A video was made featuring the players and soldiers with Ian Holloway doing the voice-over, a recital of 'In Flanders Fields', a war poem written during the First World War by Canadian physician Lieutenant Colonel John McCrae.

Reading the poem was probably one of the most difficult things the gaffer ever did.

In 1914, millions of men and women gave up their daily lives to save a nation. Football clubs across the country had players volunteer for active service, many of whom never returned.

✳ ✳ ✳ ✳ ✳

WE WERE told to treat the soldiers who had lost limbs like anybody else. They loved the banter and we had to give them plenty of it, but they were more than capable of holding their own. Such humour helps soldiers who lose limbs to keep their spirits up, especially in the darkest of days.

There is always gallows humour even in sad situations and we were informed that one soldier, who lost both legs in Afghanistan because of a land mine, was bought a foot spa by his colleagues. These sort of jokes are very much part of the team spirit that is a crucial element of the Army.

Despite what had happened to them, the soldiers joked and laughed, taking the piss out of Lee Martin's hair – an easy target, to be fair.

One guy, who was Nicky Bailey's double, had seven kids so I told him something was obviously in good working order.

Meeting the soldiers was a real eye-opener and made me realise how very lucky I am. I believe it would be beneficial to all footballers to visit places like Headley Court to see the soldiers go through their rehabilitation. Some are learning to walk again with prosthetic legs; some have no arms; some are in wheelchairs for the rest of their lives, many only in their late teens but all bearing the scars of war.

As players we take our health, our limbs and our job for granted. It is only when you go to special places such as Headley Court that it brings home how blessed we are.

To be part of the group that went to Headley Court, the video and the positive media coverage the kit generated made me extremely proud. Leading Millwall out, wearing the shirt with a poppy on it and having met our brave lads who have given so much for their country was a very special experience.

The soldiers gave the teams a guard of honour. There was I, Alan Dunne, a kid from Dublin who had become a professional footballer, captaining Millwall while guys who had lost limbs in war were effectively honouring us.

It was incredibly humbling though the soldiers were the heroes who deserved a guard of honour.

Even now, just thinking about it, makes me very emotional.

✳ ✳ ✳ ✳ ✳

AUNTIE MARIE, my dad's sister who is very close to me, came over from Ireland to watch the match. She had been a nun for 23 years before becoming a Sister – the day I was born she made her first confession. She saw the game from a box with my dad and while I was delighted to score a goal, it would have been much better had it been in a Millwall victory.

I was part of a three-man defence though I was pushing forward whenever I could. When the ball broke to me I took a touch just inside the box, and saw a tiny gap where I could take a shot. I struck the ball hard and low, and it went through the legs of Brentford captain Tony Craig before hitting the net.

Afterwards TC, who had spent eight years at Millwall in two spells before rejoining them again in the summer of 2015, tried to claim an assist.

My response was, 'Shut your legs and don't go for them, son.' Typically, he laughed it off and we still joke about it today.

The players were each given two shirts, one was auctioned by the club, the other was for ourselves. I got the team who played that day to sign my shirt with my signature on my number. I still have the framed shirt and one day I shall auction it.

Trophies and medals will remain with me forever along with the memories. There is a limit to how long I would want to keep the shirt. The prospect of making a few quid for Help For Heroes will probably be too tempting to resist.

14

25 different Millwall managers

How I hit Rhino in the face

URING MY 23 years at Millwall there were 25 different managers, joint managers and caretakers. Ryan Giggs had two managers in 24 years as a player at Manchester United. While Mick McCarthy was in charge of the first team when a ten-year-old Alan Dunne joined Millwall, the first manager I can remember is Billy Bonds who arrived in the summer of 1997, but he lasted only one season as the side struggled in the old Second Division.

We rarely saw the first team apart from during school holidays when we were invited to train at Calmont Road, Bromley, although separately from the seniors, of course. One day, I was watching them train and the ball was kicked over towards me. Alex Rae came across and whistled before saying in his deep Scottish accent, 'Pass me the ball, kid.'

For me, it was a wow moment. I was in awe of such a big Millwall star speaking to me, even more so after he said, 'Thanks.'

When I was about 14 a select few schoolboys were allowed to train with the first team and afterwards Bonds decided to take the squad, including ourselves, on a run around the training ground. I have never stopped during a run in my career – well, not since then. He had us running round the pitch for what seemed an eternity with Bonds leading the way.

For him, a marathon was a sprint and I remember looking at his legs that were like giant redwood trees, with muscles on his muscles and veins on veins. I stopped once, but continued and at the end slowly made my weary way towards the changing rooms via the gym where Bonds was on a bench lifting dumbbells. He had to be the fittest 50-year-old in the world.

Bonds, of course, made his name at West Ham where he spent 27 years as a player and manager. In those days, having claret and blue in your DNA was not the sin it has grown to be – after all, Harry Cripps, a true Millwall great, began his career with West Ham.

The rivalry has become gradually worse, more intense over the past 15 years and playing in matches against West Ham leaves a Millwall player in no doubt as to the feelings between the two sets of fans.

When you play for Millwall the inner passion is always high, but on the occasions West Ham are the opposition this goes up a few notches.

Bonds did not experience the immediate hatred many Millwall fans showed for Steve Lomas when he was appointed to follow Kenny Jackett.

Lomas had spent seven years with West Ham as a player and by 2013 any association with the club was deemed totally unacceptable in the eyes of Millwall loyalists.

The day he joined the club, one Millwall fan put up a banner at The Den with 'Fuck off Lomas' on it. After seeing that, I realised it was going to be all uphill for him, but I had to admire his balls.

*　*　*　*　*

THE FIRST Millwall legend to manage the club full-time was Billy Bonds's successor, Keith Stevens, who played 546 games in 19 years, a total beaten only by Barry Kitchener (595) – Kitch was caretaker manager for a month in 1982, by coincidence the year I was born.

Stevens's nickname is Rhino, though whether this was given because of his no-nonsense way of tackling or his nose I still don't know, but his mum was often called Mrs Rhino. Either way, Keith Stevens is always Rhino to Millwall supporters.

Rhino and then Rhino and Alan McLeary (jointly) were in charge while I was in the youth team. Millwall fans who saw Rhino play regard him as an all-time great, someone respected who had given everything for the club.

They were the two who pushed me towards the first team, but I made a huge mistake the first time I met Rhino.

I was 16 and had just left school. On my first day I was given a new training kit and a squad number – 45 in my case. I was allocated my two players to look after for the season, Nigel Spink and Lucas Neill.

This included making sure their kit and towel were laid out ready for them every morning and their boots were spotless.

There was a jobs rota for the YTS boys, which also included cleaning the changing rooms and toilets plus washing and drying the dishes and every morning and afternoon carrying goals to and from the training field.

One summer we were even called in to paint the training ground.

While football has moved on from those days, I still believe doing such chores helps you learn your trade and pushes you in that one day someone may clean your boots.

The first-teamers were stars to me, so cleaning their boots was not exactly the worst job I could have had.

I also enjoyed the £50 Christmas bonus from some of them, though Spink and Neill never gave me anything, the tight fuckers.

Anyway, on my first day as a boot cleaner I was so nervous. I had been in the building for only ten minutes when I walked past the man himself – Rhino. I knew him as the hardest of the hard central defenders of his era and I'd been told his playing style was reflected in the way he managed. In an act of supreme stupidity and naivety, trying to break the ice I said to him, 'All right, mate?'

His reply left me in no doubt that this should never be repeated.

He looked straight through me and said, 'I am not your fucking mate. I am "boss". Don't fucking forget that.'

I melted. Okay, sorry boss. Message received and understood, boss. I saw my Millwall future riding off into the sunset. I'd been there one day and the gaffer hated me. My career was over before it had started.

It was a rookie error though I thought that being at Millwall as a YTS was going to be like school, where everyone was your mate. However, my defence that no one had told me I should call him gaffer or boss is not the strongest.

Maybe it was because I didn't get off to the best of starts that I never felt comfortable with Rhino. Each time I talked to him I felt he was going to bite my head off. He had a particular tone to his voice and was usually very brief with what he said. He looked right through you and when I walked past him I was in fear, thinking, 'Please don't talk to me...please don't talk to me.'

Rhino's pre-season training was designed to really test you mentally and physically, with running and more running, putting miles in your legs, training the body and mind never to quit.

He was old school and always looking for you to show a weakness.

Rhino was manager for the 1998/99 season with McLeary his assistant. The following season McLeary was made joint-manager, but it never worked out for them. They were sacked in September 2000 after Millwall had failed to win promotion back to Division One, a sad way for it to end for them as they had played a collective total of almost 1,000 games for Millwall.

The late Ray Harford and Steve Gritt assumed control for two games, with a 100 per cent record, before Mark McGhee took over when Millwall were ninth in Division Two. Promotion was achieved eight months later with a club record 93 points, though Rhino and Macca would no doubt say it was their team.

McGhee was the manager who handed me my Millwall debut so I shall always respect him for the chance he gave me. On 19 March 2002 I came on as an 18-year-old substitute for

Stephen McPhail in the 67th minute against Sheffield United at Bramall Lane when Millwall were leading 1-0.

Within 30 seconds Michael Tonge cut inside me and made it 1-1.

I remember the music that United played when they scored – 'Tom Hark' by the Piranhas – and at that moment I wanted to disappear to another planet. All I could think was, 'They have scored, it was my fault, my career's finished.' That tune haunted me for years after.

Stuart Nethercott put us ahead again and my confidence rose, but 'Tom Hark' was played twice more after two goals in the final three minutes by Peter Ndlovu.

I left the field convinced I was not ready for the big time and wondering if I would ever be good enough to play at that level.

I had to wait almost a year for my full debut which came on 15 February 2003 in a 2-0 home defeat by Reading.

McGhee was a very clever and wealthy guy thanks to his successful businesses and would arrive for training in a 7 Series BMW. He was a top player in Scotland with Aberdeen and still looked useful in training. I got on well with him, he was very sharp with his banter and he really believed in me, pushing me to do well.

It was while McGhee was in charge that I was the most worried I have ever been in my career.

* * * * *

IT STARTED when Paul Robinson and I had been on a night out during pre-season in Sweden and missed the 10am coach to training. We both thought we had set our alarms when in fact neither of us had. I believed Robbo was the sensible one of the pair of us and would definitely have set his alarm.

I remember waking up, looking at the time on my phone and shouting, 'Robbo – get the fuck up. We're late.'

We sprinted down four flights of stairs, hoping the lads had not left. They had and neither of us knew where the training ground was. We had to sit in the lobby waiting for what felt like an eternity for the coach to return. We were so scared we didn't say a word to each other.

Missing training is serious and we were terrified of the consequences. When the manager returned he walked straight past us which made us even more horrified of what might happen. We followed him and spoke to him before he got in the lift.

'Gaffer, we're sorry. We forgot to set our alarms.'

He replied as the lift doors closed, 'I'll see you two at lunch.'

Luckily, Mark McGhee probably realised it was a youthful mistake, but no way were we going to be let off lightly.

It was decided at lunch there would be a court case after dinner to decide our fate. We were so worried that we would be fined a week's wages or even sent home that neither Robbo nor I could eat a thing.

Steve Claridge said he would be the prosecutor and Dave Tuttle thought it would be amusing to defend us which proved not to be the easiest task. In fairness, our claim that we both thought the other had set his alarm after a night on the lash was hardly 'beyond all reasonable doubt' evidence Tuttle could argue on our behalf.

However, he was still the world's worst defence barrister and thank goodness we weren't paying him.

The jury comprised a few of the senior players including Paul Ifill, Neil Harris, Steven Reid and Sean Dyche, who not only had to decide whether we were guilty – it probably took them three seconds to make up their minds – they also had to choose our inevitable punishment.

We didn't mind anything as long as we weren't fined. We pleaded guilty and apologised, hoping we would be let off with just a warning.

No chance.

Their conclusion was that for the five remaining days of the trip Paul and I had to be everyone's bitch. Looking back, we would have taken the fine of a week's wages.

Whenever any of the lads wanted something from a shop, which was a ten-minute walk from the hotel, we had to fetch it. We had to clean everyone's boots before and after training. Room service? Just ask Dunney or Robbo. We had to go down to the kitchen and take it up to them. Basically we were their unpaid skivvies.

On top of all that, we also had extra running in training. We were young lads and had to be taught a lesson. I can smile now, but delivering four successive room services to laughing team-mates did not seem too funny at the time.

McGhee left the club in October 2003 though we were eighth in the old Division One. His last game in charge was against Preston at home on a Tuesday night which we lost 1-0 and I played on the left wing. Because I was quick he thought I could do a job anywhere.

I was gutted to see him leave, but his successor was a man who lit up The Den with his personality.

❋　❋　❋　❋　❋

FOR TEAM SPIRIT and lifting morale there was no better manager than Dennis Wise who led us to the 2004 FA Cup Final against Manchester United.

I think we would have been promoted to the Premier League had it not been for our FA Cup run. We smashed West Ham 4-1 at The Den in March and we were flying, but after defeating Sunderland in the semi-finals we took only six out of the remaining 24 points available.

Two or three of our top players, particularly, became sidetracked by the final because of the huge media attention, plus the fear of injury or suspension which saw our form dip.

Wise had been there, seen it, done it and won it. He was the biggest name I had seen at The Den, the respect he commanded was immediate and absolute.

While Wise had a disciplinary record that had kept the Football Association constantly busy, his personality and willingness to do whatever it took to win made him an ideal fit for Millwall. When he didn't get his own way he could be a nasty bastard, but I liked the self-belief that contributed towards him being such a successful player.

Wisey could never be fooled and hated lies. He would say, 'Just tell me the truth.'

On a pre-season tour of Canada, Curtis Weston found out the hard way that if you were caught lying to Wisey you would regret it.

We had our one official night out, but there was always an unofficial one. On the unofficial night out we planned our meeting and getaway points so that staff would not know what was going on.

The trouble is, they always knew.

Having trained the next morning and stupidly believing we'd got away with our so-called secret night out, we were heading for a welcome shower when Wisey called us all together. He said, 'Listen lads, everyone who went out last night please step to the left.'

About 20 of us, me included, moved to the left leaving two players. One was Darren Ward who was probably busy counting his pumpkin seeds. The other was Weston.

Forever one step ahead, Wisey was probably aware of what anyone had done before he even did it. Wisey knew every trick in the book because he invented many of them.

He said to the guilty 20, 'I know you were out and I'm not happy, but at least you told the truth. You are all going to do five 800m runs.'

Turning to Weston, he said, 'As for you, I know you were out. Don't ever fucking lie to me again.'

Weston had lost his credit for pleading not guilty and three extra runs were added to his sentence which, in 90 degrees after a night on the piss, was not easy.

Looking back at our tour of Canada, it was more like a stag do than a pre-season.

One evening after dinner in a restaurant, Dave Livermore and I had to play the spoon-in-the-mouth game where you put the handle of the spoon in your mouth and have to try to hit the other on the top of the head with the round end. I found it difficult to get a decent hit on Livermore, yet he constantly found my head which was like a boiled egg being cracked.

In the end, I had to give up because I wouldn't have been able to head the ball the next day. Only then did I discover somebody was behind me with a spoon in his hand whacking it on the top of my head.

The next victim was Peter Sweeney. He was told by Kevin Muscat, 'You can hide a pound coin anywhere on your body and within ten seconds I will find it. If not, you can have the money that is in the whip.'

While Sweeney was carefully placing the pound coin among his crown jewels, Muzzy went outside so he could not see what was happening. What Sweeney didn't know was that Muzzy had put his thumbs in a car's exhaust pipe.

He returned and started by putting his dirty thumbs on Sweeney's forehead and then down his cheeks as if he was trying to read his mind. Muzzy then said, 'I bet the coin is down there,' and Sweeney owned up that it was.

However, Sweeney was unaware that for an hour he had black thumb prints over his face and it was only when he went to the toilet he realised what had happened. I don't think I have ever laughed so much in my life.

Under Wisey, we worked hard and played hard, but the team spirit was top-class.

AFTER Dennis Wise came Steve Claridge for five weeks – he never took charge of a competitive match. With the club in turmoil following the resignation of Theo Paphitis, who stayed on as a director, Jeff Burnige became chairman for two months in which time I managed to negotiate a new two-year contract with him.

Burnige is Millwall through and through, and his father Herbert was a previous chairman.

While he was a member of the board, Burnige was still able to join in the players' banter and one night, on a pre-season tour, we knew he was going out with the staff to have a few sociable drinks, as they do.

After we had eaten dinner a couple of the lads obtained his room key from reception (don't ask). Every loose piece of furniture was crammed into the bathroom; the bed, chair, lamp, pictures, powder was put in his shoes and the arms cut off a shirt.

It went a bit too far, but it was just typical footballers, always looking for a cheap laugh.

The next morning we were on the coach when Burnige arrived. There wasn't a straight face among the players and fair do's to JB, he entered into the spirit of things and said, 'I came back last night, I'd had a few drinks, went to my room and thought I'd sit down to take my shoes off. I went to sit on the chair, but it wasn't there.

'I managed to get my shoes, shirt and trousers off and decided to go to sleep. Only one problem, there was no fucking bed either.

'I don't care what you did or who done it, but can I ask one thing? Please, please, whoever nicked my shoelaces, can I please have them back?'

Burnige was standing there in a shirt with no arms and all he wanted was his shoelaces.

He took it really well, though I can't remember seeing him on a pre-season trip again.

PETER DE SAVARY took over from Jeff Burnige as chairman with Colin Lee becoming our third manager in as many months.

For some reason, many people didn't like Lee, though I had no problems with him. The chaotic goings-on at board level unsettled the club and Millwall were unable to climb away from the lower reaches of the Championship in the first half of 2005/06 so Lee was moved upstairs to become director of football.

Dave Tuttle and then Alan McLeary with Tony Burns had four months in control, but on 17 April 2006 relegation to League 1 was confirmed with a 2-0 loss at Southampton. The 13 goals Millwall scored at home was the second lowest total in Football League history.

In August 2006 it was the turn of Nigel Spackman, the least impressive manager I played under. Five years after being sacked by Barnsley he was in charge at The Den for seven weeks – 12 games and two wins.

Spackman was way out of his depth. He offered very little, he was poor tactically and struggled to command authority. The players sensed weakness from the day he arrived, but he was never cut out to be the manager of Millwall.

When he moved on we were 23rd in League 1 and Willie Donachie, who was assistant to Spackman, was promoted to manager. We finished 2006/07 in mid-table.

Donachie was a little different, an unusual guy, someone who was more into the mental side of the game. He also loved his yoga and breathing patterns. He was not the greatest tactician, but it was difficult not to like him and he was very good to me. Donachie always played me, many times in midfield, and he also gave me a new contract. I have only fond memories of him and great respect for him as a man.

When Donachie left, we were in a bad place. Players were arguing, excuses after excuses were being made, everyone was blaming each other. We struggled to find the confidence that is so essential in football. This tended to affect everybody's self-belief and back-stabbing became commonplace.

The club was at the lowest I had ever seen it.

People may say the manager is ultimately responsible for this, but Donachie was in charge for little over a year and inherited a situation where the club had signed too many players while too many had too much to say.

It would have been difficult for anyone to come in and find an immediate cure for all the ills that were festering. Donachie did his best, but there were so many big egos he was facing a losing battle.

Richard Shaw and Colin West took the reins for one match. Two days after a game is usually a warm-down…a light stretch and a jog for those who had played.

Shaw and West had us doing pitch runs. My head went after about seven and I told them, 'Fuck this, I'm going in.'

I was called in to see them afterwards and West gave me the biggest load of bollocks I'd ever heard, but sadly it ultimately proved effective. He said, 'I'm going to fine you £400 because what you did does not set a good example.'

While I didn't necessarily disagree with him, I felt the fine was very harsh, not to mention random.

Knowing he wouldn't be in charge for much longer, I refused to pay it.

West's reply to this was a blinder, but it worked and I paid the fine.

He said, 'Dunney – I know you're a good lad, but there will be a new manager coming in here during the next few days. I don't want him coming in and asking, "What's Dunney like?" and me having to say, "Mmm, not sure about him."'

I liked West, but this was a form of football blackmail. He was saying if I didn't cough up the dosh he'd cast immediate doubts about me to the new boss.

I could not call his bluff.

The next day, with extreme reluctance, I handed over the £400 in cash – crisp pinkies, too. I was told it would be put in the safe – a safe I had never seen before.

After West and Shaw, Kenny Jackett started his five and a half years in charge. I didn't know much about Jackett, but the club did well to bring in someone who was experienced in how to win promotion from the lower leagues.

15

I had to beg Jackett so I could propose to Aimee

He was not impressed by my jeweller

'CAN I see you, please, Alan? In my office.'

As a footballer, it is something you do not want to hear from the manager. It rarely means good news and in my case it certainly wasn't good.

This was not so much a request as an order by Kenny Jackett towards the end of the 2007/08 season, his first in charge at Millwall.

His opening sentence could not have been more to the point.

Jackett said, 'You are not part of my plans, find another club.'

I had a year remaining on my contract, yet in that moment my whole career seemed doomed. I had never heard this before. I was gutted as I left his office. I saw out the remainder of the season, training with the development squad and when I went on a family holiday to Florida I did some serious thinking, wondering what I had done wrong, but basically feeling sorry for myself which is unusual for me.

Upon returning home, I received a phonecall from Jackett. Right-back Danny Senda had been injured in the last game of the season and would miss the start of the following campaign which proved to be a fortunate break for me.

Jackett said, 'Alan, come back for pre-season training and I'll give you another chance. I want you to play right-back for me.'

Joe Gallen, his assistant, had told the manager that I had played more than 200 games 'so he obviously has to have something'.

I have no idea why Jackett said what he said, only he knows that. I was unsure how to take it, but it was the wake-up call I needed. If his motive was to generate a response from me, it worked. I was comfortable at Millwall, perhaps a little too comfortable, and I never thought a manager would tell me to find another club. I was wrong.

*　*　*　*　*

KENNY JACKETT and I did not get off to the best of starts. I don't think he understood me, maybe I was a bit too complacent which he did not like in his squad.

However, Jackett was such an experienced, determined manager and he got my career back on track. He gave me a different view, not just on football. He was not only a football manager, he was like a life coach, too. I learned so much from him and I would not have achieved what I did had it not been for his advice and the one-on-one chats.

I returned for pre-season training as fit as I could be and put more into it than ever before. I wanted to show Jackett what I could do, what I was capable of, impress upon him I was his best right-back and that he had made the correct decision to give me another chance.

When I look back, I realise I was not working as hard as I could because I didn't need to, I was not as professional as my job demanded and Jackett knew this.

He wanted players who were desperate to play, desperate to win and desperate to succeed.

Every single day he hammered this message home to the players in a way that no previous manager had. Whenever he spoke to us, whether it was about tactics or anything, 'desire' was always mentioned. Many times. He demanded that we had the burning desire to want to succeed.

I remember being in a meeting with him and he said, 'Don't let your career just fade out. Don't become a nobody. Put in the graft now and you'll be a better player and make a good career for yourself.'

I felt he belatedly saw something in me and was keen for me to fulfil my potential. Jackett also believed I could be a top coach or manager one day. I didn't so much go that extra yard, but an extra two yards and Jackett began to trust me in a way he had not previously done.

I think I altered his opinion of me by becoming a better professional, while being part of a winning team also helped his views of me to slowly change.

His knowledge, passion and drive for the game were infectious. The way he would dissect a match on the way home was not just a coaching masterclass, his enthusiasm was a credit to his profession.

Yes, he was ruthless in his quest for success and would give a player very few chances. Yes, if any player's performances and professionalism were not at Jackett's level then he was on his way out.

Yet very few who worked with Jackett would say a bad word about him.

Like previous managers, Jackett signed a number of right-backs to either replace me or provide competition, depending on how you look at such things. He told me on many occasions, sometimes on a Friday, 'I'm bringing someone in tomorrow, a right-back.'

I somehow managed to see them all off and was always confident of coming through any challenge for my position.

Millwall is a tough club to play for and many players cannot cope with such pressures.

You have to realise what the club is all about – Millwall is different to other clubs and I understood its history, the supporters, what it means to the fans, the demands and expectations.

In his last season at The Den when I thought I was playing well, to my surprise Jackett pulled me aside and told me Adam Smith was joining on loan from Spurs, a player Millwall had been watching for a while.

He said, 'Dunney, I know you've had many right-backs to compete with in the past and you will no doubt have more in the future, so this is nothing new for you. It's something you'll have to deal with for the rest of your career. I know you have never let me down. I just need to try something different, something more attacking, someone who can bring the ball out from the back.'

In football this is one of the worst feelings, when you are told somebody is coming in to potentially replace you. It makes you feel so little, so embarrassed and you start doubting your ability.

At times like this it takes someone strong-willed and strong-minded to not lie down and concede defeat.

I had faced such a challenge so many times in my career that in the end I almost started to enjoy it, wondering who the next player brought in would be. I became more confident each time a new right-back came in because I had been there before and knew I had something special in me, the Millwall lion spirit, that others did not possess.

In 2012/13 Smith and I both made 25 league appearances and at the start of the following season he moved to Derby on loan.

For all the new right-backs he brought in, I was still given three contracts by Jackett, the first two for one year and the third for three years. He made me work for them and in the end I like to think we had a good relationship over the time he was there, even though we had our differences.

Nothing serious, but many a time he told me to fuck off.

I REMEMBER one pre-season trip to Dublin under Kenny Jackett. We were allowed our traditional night out so we headed for the Temple Bar area where there are many bars though I have yet to see one temple.

I say night out, we actually left our hotel at three in the afternoon. Our curfew was midnight so we had to be back on the coach by 11.

We all headed for a tour around the Guinness factory and when you reach the top you are offered a free pint. For some reason tickets kept appearing from David Forde's pocket – you'd think he worked there. After taking advantage of every last free Guinness ticket we could find, we headed to the city centre.

By eight o'clock and after one too many pints of the black stuff I thought it would be funny to do my signature handstand outside the pub we had just been to.

Unsurprisingly, it turned out not to be the good idea me and Arthur Guinness had initially thought.

Apart from my money, mobile phone and goodness knows what else falling out of my pockets, Jackett and Joe Gallen walked by at the precise moment I was displaying my gymnastic skills. Any hope I had of the boss being impressed by his multi-talented full-back disappeared when, on the coach back to the hotel and again at breakfast, Jackett said, 'A handstand…a handstand outside a pub,' shaking his head as he spoke.

This was not the last time the handstand was mentioned, either. You just can't do a handstand outside a bar in Dublin without being seen by your manager.

Everyone made it back to the coach by 11 and Jackett was first off the bus upon arriving at the hotel. For some reason he just walked in, not looking behind him. We followed the boss to the reception and as he disappeared towards the lift we turned round and took taxis back to Temple Bar.

To search for a temple, of course.

Ireland was Jackett's favourite place for pre-season training. We would stay at the superb Portmarnock Hotel, which the national team also used. The facilities were top drawer and the gaffer liked it because there was a golf course and it was very quiet.

One year in Dublin, Fordey and I missed the 11pm coach by a minute, but managed to hail a cab to follow the team back to the hotel. Luckily we arrived just behind the coach and walked in innocently with the other players.

Another year, we had to leave the hotel at 6.30am for an early flight. Me, Zak Whitbread and Gary Alexander had returned from our night out at five to six and believed we should have 20 minutes' sleep before our departure which would refresh us.

How wrong can you be?

We awoke feeling as rough as it is humanly possible to feel. We stuffed everything in our bags, jumped on them, zipped them up as best we could and made our way to the coach.

As we boarded – needless to say we were the last on – the players were laughing because they knew what had happened. I remember Jackett looking at me, my eyes were like two fried eggs in a bucket of blood. I so did not want what remained of my eyes to make contact with the boss's, but inevitably they did.

When the coach pulled away I glanced over at the hotel lobby where my training gear and much else was on the floor, proof, if it were needed, that I had not zipped up my bag properly.

Mind you, it is not only players who can over-indulge. On our pre-season tour of Canada some of us arrived back at the hotel at 3am, our guilt lessened by the sight of one of our big-name coaches being carried out of a taxi.

Dublin is my home city and even though I can remember little of my life there having moved to England when I was two, I remain Irish through and through. Irish pubs are ideal for socialising, if not handstands, though a friend of mine from south-east London was puzzled when he heard a local ordering a 'Shirley Bassey' in a bar in the Irish capital.

He could not think of any drink to rhyme with Shirley Bassey, so next time he was at the bar he asked what it was. 'A Shirley Bassey,' said the bartender. 'You don't know what it is?'

Pointing to the whiskey, he said, 'It's a Black Bush.'

✳ ✳ ✳ ✳ ✳

AT MILLWALL our schedule for the following month was made known midway through the month. When I found out what the plans were for October 2008 I booked to take my girlfriend of six years, Aimee, who was approaching the big 3-0, to Paris for the night as a special birthday present and also a very special surprise.

I planned to propose to Aimee in the most romantic city in the world.

Three weeks before the big day and knowing we were off on the Wednesday, the date of her birthday, I booked two first-class tickets on Eurostar, plus a top hotel with dinner at The Ritz. A jeweller friend from Hatton Garden – more of whom later – had made a ring with the date of the engagement engraved on it.

Yes, what a wonderful idea you are no doubt thinking.

The day before we were due to leave for Paris, Kenny Jackett told us a reserve game had been rescheduled for the Wednesday. I would be needed for the match.

Panic. How could I be in two places at the same time?

Once the schedules were pinned up, they very rarely changed. But 6 October 2008 was the exception.

I went to see the gaffer and explained my predicament. There was a silence as he paused for a minute, which felt like an hour. I thought he was going to say, 'Like fuck you're going to Paris.'

But he was very understanding and told me to go rather than play for the reserves, adding with a smile, 'She'd better say yes.'

So there I was in The Ritz with Aimee. I waited until all the other customers had gone which seemed to take forever. Aimee had no idea of what was to come.

The big moment eventually arrived. Yours truly went down on one knee and asked Aimee to marry me.

After saying 'yes' she cried her eyes out. When the bill came I cried my eyes out, too.

After her tears had been wiped away I told Aimee what had nearly happened.

The gaffer was pleased when I came in on the Thursday and told him there was a happy ending and not a wasted trip.

* * * * *

BACK TO MY jeweller friend, who also sold watches – all legit, he's not Del Boy. One Monday afternoon when things were quiet I invited him to the training ground to see if any of the lads wanted to buy a top-of-the-range watch at a decent price.

My pal arrived wearing a tracksuit with a gym bag containing loads of designer watches. Someone at reception came to find me and I showed him in, sat him down and brought him a Bill Roffey (coffee). He had Rolex, Tag and Cartier, all the top brands, and the players, young and old, were suitably impressed.

Then Kenny Jackett walked past and I could see the look in his eye.

He was far from impressed as he went into his office. A few minutes later I was told, 'The gaffer wants to see you upstairs.'

When I walked in his face was red with anger.

'Who the fuck is that?'

'Sorry gaffer, he's a friend of mine. He came to see if any of the lads wanted to buy a watch. He'd give us a good price.'

'Fucking watches? What is this? A fucking Christmas club?'

'Tell that geezer to get his stuff and get the fuck out of my training ground. You're supposed to be setting an example. Those young boys down there look up to you and you are trying to get them to buy watches. What sort of example is that? You should be telling them to buy [he pointed at his own wrist] one of these. Get a £10 watch and buy a flat instead of a Rolex.'

'I have a flat, gaffer.'

'Go and buy another fucking flat.'

What was said filtered back to the lads who gave me some stick, but Jackett laughed about it in the end. My pal did not make any sales and he had to leave, without making his excuses. The training ground was for football, not selling watches. It was unprofessional of me and Jackett was right to tear a strip off me.

Another run-in concerned the club's awards night which was traditionally held during the week before the final game of the season. On the Monday after the last game we would

My first Millwall goal against Gillingham at the Den in October, 2004. I dedicated the goal to my mum.

Millwall's 2004 FA Cup Final squad. It was suit-fitting day and we also recorded the cup final song. The Jeff Banks suits were definitely better than our version of Dean Martin's 'Volare'.

Millwall v Scunthorpe United, Wembley, May, 2009. My main memory of the League One play-off final was the 100-plus degree heat and almost having my eyebrows singed by the flame-throwers on the way out to the pitch.

Mr and Mrs Dunne on our wedding day, June 19, 2009 at the beautiful Chewton Glen Hotel in the New Forest, Hampshire.

Celebrating the last-minute equaliser against Walsall in March, 2010. It was chosen as Goal of the Season by Millwall fans.

Millwall's Player of the Year 2009/10. Being selected for the award by the wonderful Millwall supporters was a highlight of my career.

Kenny Jackett with the 2010 League One playoff trophy. Kenny was the manager I learned most from.

My testimonial against Charlton Athletic in July, 2011. It was one of my proudest moments and I was delighted to walk out with my two children Lola and Shay. It was also the only time I have ever been applauded by a referee.

With Richard Chaplow and David Forde in Marbella. I attempted to play golf and then drew the short straw with the cigars.

Me, Tommy Pratt, Gary Alexander and David Forde in St Tropez for Tommy's Big 4-oh. We were joined by Frank Maloney – now Kellie. It was the last time I saw him as Frank.

Red is the new orange. Sent off at Brighton in August 2013 for a second cautionable offence. My defence counsel of Nicky Bailey, Shaun Derry and Danny Shittu were unsuccessful.

Outside the Dorchester Hotel in London with Dylan Pratt, son of friend Tommy, and a fish called Fish. It was Millwall's good luck charm as we survived relegation in 2013/14 with an eight-game unbeaten run.

Challenging for the ball with Wilfried Zaha of Crystal Palace at the Den in April, 2013. I had said the winger was not worth £20 million and Palace fans have never forgiven me for this, even making up a less than flattering song in my 'honour'. Photo: Press Association

Another proud moment. Wearing the special one-off camouflage kit, I scored Millwall's second goal against Brentford on 8 November 2014 – the anniversary of my grandad Peter's death. My dad Paul and auntie Marie were at the match during memorial weekend. I dedicated my Man of the Match trophy to my auntie to put on my grandad's grave in Dublin.

Ian Holloway congratulates me after we finally broke our Birmingham City hoodoo with a 1-0 win over Blues in February, 2015. I scored the only goal in the 51st minute – a sweet feeling.

Team Dunne at the Den. Shay, Lola, Aimee and a very proud husband/father.

report to the training ground and after that we were free to go on holiday. With this in mind, in the March I had booked a holiday with Aimee in Dubai, departing on the Tuesday evening. What could go wrong? How about everything.

Two weeks before we were due to fly to Dubai it was announced the end of season awards night would be on the Tuesday after the final game, the Tuesday when we were scheduled to leave for the Middle East.

I went to see the gaffer and explained my situation, 'I've booked two tickets costing £1,500 and the tickets have been issued.'

Jackett paused for a few seconds, as was his habit, and I sensed from his facial contortions what was coming. I was not wrong.

'Why didn't you fucking ask me before you planned anything? You can't book anything until you speak to me. I might have wanted you in for fitness testing.'

'But we've never been in after the Monday...'

'You have to go? It'll cost you two weeks' wages.'

A quick calculation – which would be the more expensive, the fine or the flights?

In one ear, I had my wife saying I could not go to the awards night, in the other the manager was telling me I could not go on holiday. Heads I lose, tails I lose.

I told the gaffer I would try to change the tickets, but Aimee reminded me that we had arranged for our kids to be taken care of from the Tuesday. I decided to go for the sympathy vote and went back to see the manager for a second time.

'Gaffer, this is no joke. I really have to go. Look, here are the tickets [which I'd printed out]. If you want to fine me two weeks' wages then I'll have to pay it.'

The feel-sorry-for-me approach failed miserably.

'I said I can fine you a minimum of two weeks' wages, but I could fine you more.'

Fuck that, I thought, and walked out, slamming the door.

I attended the awards dinner the next night, having lost money – I don't even want to think how much – on the flights. Aimee was not happy, which is putting it mildly, but she understood, I think.

I may have had a few altercations with the gaffer, but they were quickly forgotten and we remained close.

* * * * *

THE MILLWALL fans loved Kenny Jackett. He'd taken the club to Wembley three times and led them back to the Championship when we won the League 1 play-offs in 2010 by beating Swindon in the final.

We finished ninth in our first season back in the Championship while three years later we reached the semi-finals of the FA Cup, losing 2-0 to the eventual winners, Wigan Athletic.

Jackett spent little money during his five and a half years at The Den and when results were not going Millwall's way, the chairman, John Berylson, always backed his manager for which he deserves credit.

In the end, Jackett had taken the club as far as he could. There was a natural ending to his time at Millwall, where he will be remembered as one of the best managers in our history. When he left, I texted him, 'I am sorry to see you go, but I cannot thank you enough for all you did for me. You put my career back on track.'

His reply was emotional and I shall always have huge respect for the man.

Jackett was given a standing ovation by The Den faithful when he returned with Wolves in October 2014. He is not one to glory in attention, but I had a smile on my face watching him as he walked to the visiting dug-out.

I shook his hand after the game, but as usual he had kept himself to himself before the kick-off. I have the utmost respect for my old gaffer though at the same time never have I played in a game where I wanted to win so badly. I knew how desperately Jackett wanted to beat his former club. Of course, he is desperate to win every match, an emotion he instilled in me when he was at Millwall.

Jackett would have used his inside knowledge of the players he knew from his time in charge to Wolves' advantage. If the start of his comeback went well, Jackett would not have been happy with the way his team threw away a 3-0 lead, though we showed the sort of spirit he would have admired by scoring three times in the last 23 minutes to draw 3-3.

Joe Gallen, his assistant who was with Jackett at Millwall, said to me afterwards, 'We didn't deserve to be three goals up in the first place.'

When you lead by three goals, you think you must win. I'm told it was the first time Millwall had come back from a 3-0 deficit at The Den since being three behind against Wigan in August 1999.

While we celebrated what seemed like a victory, Jackett would have ripped into his team in their dressing room.

✳   ✳   ✳   ✳   ✳

ON THE DAY Kenny Jackett left Millwall, I was called to an emergency meeting along with Paul Robinson and Danny Shittu to talk to John Berylson and the board so they could gauge our feelings about the way forward for Millwall. My view was that we should not go for a young manager, that we needed someone with experience.

A month later Steve Lomas, who had been in charge of St Johnstone for less than two years, was appointed.

An inexperienced manager who had played for West Ham. It was certainly a very brave decision, though I failed to work out the thought process behind it. My view was that because of Lomas's West Ham connection it was always going to blow up, no matter how well he did. The collective finger of The Den faithful was on the trigger.

Lomas did not get off to the best of starts as Millwall manager. He phoned me shortly before we were due to report back and said he hoped to take us to Portugal or Dubai for pre-season training. A big early plus mark for the new manager and a reward for the team for reaching the semi-finals of the FA Cup.

Word spread and when we were asked to report back three days earlier than scheduled nobody minded, especially with a potential trip to somewhere exotic. It turned out that we were going to prepare for the new season somewhere less attractive than Portugal or Dubai.

The University of Warwick in Coventry.

Instead of a week training and enjoying the delights of Dubai or the pleasures of Portugal we had the less than wonderful wonders of Warwick for a week.

They included a room with a single bed, no telephone, no wifi and no atmosphere. The lads were so disappointed and it was a terrible start for Lomas even if it was not totally his fault. It was a mistake mentioning a sunshine location and then being sent to Coventry – literally.

While the facilities to train were excellent, there was little else to do and no opportunity for everyone to go on the traditional bonding night out.

Despite the calamity of Coventry, I liked Lomas, a council estate lad with a good sense of humour and a thick skin. He had to have some balls to accept the Millwall job, given his background, which I admired and respected. I'm not sure if this was a two-way street because I don't think he ever trusted me, there always seemed to be some tension whenever we spoke.

Perhaps it was because I had been with the club for so long and Millwall were part of me. While on the surface we got on, I felt any conversation between us was empty and false.

We'd had an altercation after I was sent off for a challenge on him when he was with Queens Park Rangers, but I don't think that was an issue. I believe the Millwall job came too early for Lomas – he was 39 at the time – while he was always fighting a losing battle because of his West Ham career.

Neil Harris and Scott Fitzgerald were joint caretaker managers for three games, but the board took little time in finding a permanent manager.

If the club made a mistake by appointing Lomas, the man they chose to succeed him was the experienced Ian Holloway.

16

Joker Ollie was famous for his one-liners

Yet he was one of the most seriousmanagers I knew

IAN HOLLOWAY'S sacking pleased many Millwall fans who blamed him for another, ultimately unsuccessful, season of battling against relegation.

I would not totally point the finger of failure at the gaffer. The quality of some players Holloway had was not good enough.

The players he brought in were not good enough either and he has to take the blame for that.

Recruitment was poor and while there weren't many players available to him, too many of those who were signed turned out to be poor decisions.

The club took a £250,000 gamble on Lee Gregory, who had been a prolific goalscorer with Halifax Town in the Conference North and Conference Premier, but he found Championship defences a more difficult nut to crack. It was a lot of pressure for Gregory in his first season in league football to be our main goal threat and it was unfair for Millwall to rely so much on him.

You can have an honest team of players all giving 100 per cent, but if the right balance is not there you will fail which Millwall did.

We had lost Carlos Edwards and Nicky Bailey, two big players, to long-term injuries and they were never replaced adequately. Crucially, we did not have a striker who could be relied upon to score regularly. Our clean sheets record was good enough for Millwall to have finished mid-table, but our goals for record was awful and was the main reason for relegation.

I had the impression Millwall wanted to stabilise in 2014/15 and go for it the following season. But you can't do that because the Championship is too good for that sort of approach.

Millwall began the season well, but didn't strengthen at the right time, instead hoping to hang on and push forward in 2015/16. Twenty-four players started 2014/15 with their contracts ending the following summer and I think those who had done well for the club should have had the uncertainty taken from them with the offer of a new deal sooner rather than later.

On a personal level, I thought the club should have offered me a new contract early in the season. I felt a little hurt by this, though it never affected the way I played or my belief in Millwall and, of course, no new deal was ever put on the table.

For four months we had a dysfunctional squad with tension, personal agendas, rows, back-stabbing and fights during training on a regular basis.

Holloway had to deal with all this negativity which hardly helped the battle against relegation.

Neil Harris, who had been the under-21 coach for two years, was the logical choice to steady the ship for the remaining ten games after Holloway's departure. As a Millwall legend Harris immediately had the fans onside and he felt more prepared for the job than when he was caretaker manager for a couple of weeks in December 2013 following the departure of Steve Lomas.

A notable difference between Holloway and Harris was the intensity of their team meetings. Ollie's would last for between 45 minutes and an hour each day after training. As someone who always wants to learn about football, this did not bother me. In fact, I enjoyed it.

But for many of the lads who were only really concerned about playing it was too much. Harris, in contrast, kept things simple.

Despite some heavy defeats there was never any lack of passion, fight, commitment or determination from the players.

I repeat, the team simply weren't good enough.

✳ ✳ ✳ ✳ ✳

THE REST of the squad were in the players' room at the training ground when Sky Sports News announced Ian Holloway had been sacked. A minute before the news broke on television Deano Standing, Millwall's head of media, had taken me aside to tell me Holloway had gone.

It was Tuesday 10 March 2015 – a week after Holloway had called a meeting of all players and staff to tell everyone that John Berylson, the chairman, had given him an assurance he would be in charge for the remainder of the season.

A week can be a long time in football.

We had lost 4-1 to Norwich City on the Saturday and I found it strange that the manager did not come out of the dug-out. Ollie is usually one of the liveliest, most animated characters in the technical area, but on this occasion he stayed on his seat for 90 minutes.

Maybe he didn't want to make the players nervous or add to the growing pressure on the team. Perhaps he was keeping out of the firing line from fans who had been making their feelings about Holloway very clear for weeks.

The Norwich defeat proved to be one too many for the chairman to accept. The club had brought in players over the previous two transfer windows with no real improvement. Millwall's attendances were reflected by another season of battling against relegation and Berylson felt he had to act in the best interests of the club.

While it had been a disappointing seven months, it was still something of a shock after the meeting Holloway had called seven days earlier.

I was unhappy that the manager had been sacked. He put a lot of trust and faith in me, making me captain, and I felt I had let him down. It hurt me a lot.

Yes, he made some mistakes with team selections and constantly changing the side to find a winning formula. I don't think I played in the same position more than two games in a row. He tried formations that did not work. I still believed Holloway would have got it right eventually, but he did not have the necessary ingredients that season.

The manager took a lot of stick for the poor performances of the side, never blaming the players who deserved criticism for underachieving. Ollie gave it his best shot, he could not have done more for the cause, even trying too much because in the end he looked visibly drained.

I texted the gaffer to say I felt I had let him down as his captain, telling him that he was a real, honest man who I enjoyed working with, wishing him and his wife luck for the future.

His reply must remain private, but it brought a tear to my eye.

✳　✳　✳　✳　✳

IT WAS all so different when Ian Holloway stood in front of the Millwall squad and staff in January 2014.

Around 40 sets of eyes were focused on the new manager as he addressed the players for the first time, which is one of the most challenging of jobs. The nature of the sport means there are between 30 and 40 players and staff looking at the new boss, studying his words, body language and searching for any weaknesses. If one, or more, is found, it can be an uphill struggle for the manager from there.

The players are trying to work out the manager and vice versa.

When Holloway arrived for his initial team meeting I looked him straight in the eyes and I knew right away he was a man who would gain my respect. Kenny Jackett was also able to achieve instant belief from the squad and Ollie was immediately in control as soon as he stood in front of us.

He spoke from the heart, his honesty and emotions were real. I was confident Millwall had appointed the right manager.

✴   ✴   ✴   ✴   ✴

I HAD never met Ian Holloway until he succeeded Steve Lomas. My opinion of Ollie was based on television interviews, but it can be difficult to form a view of a manager who says, 'It's all very well having a great pianist playing, but it's no good if you haven't got anyone to get the piano on the stage in the first place – otherwise the pianist would be standing there with no bloody piano to play.'

I thought he was a character, but had no idea what was behind the jokes and one-liners. In fact, Holloway is one of the most serious people I have ever met.

He had left Crystal Palace, newspapers claiming he was tired and didn't have the energy for the job. Ten weeks later he was appointed manager of a rival south-east London club after Kenny Jackett, then with Wolves, had advised Ollie to have a chat with Millwall.

Jackett told him that chairman John Berylson and chief executive Andy Ambler were good people to work for and within minutes of meeting the pair Ollie agreed that Jackett was spot on.

Holloway said that of all the clubs he had managed, none had made it more obvious than Millwall that they wanted him. He was not one of several candidates, he was the only contender which made Ollie feel a million dollars.

He knew Millwall were the club for him.

The chairman admitted he had made a mistake by appointing Lomas to take over from Jackett, but by attracting a manager like Holloway, with Premier League experience, it reflected positively on Millwall.

While he is a combination of seriousness and humour, Ollie had a temper which at times exploded.

He could be very vocal where referees were concerned, though occasionally he became so worked up he said things he later regretted. His aggression was fuelled by what he perceived as injustices against his team and I've seen him wait for the referee after the game, having to be calmed down by the coaching staff.

It is never good when your emotions get the better of you whether you are a manager or a player and in November 2014 against Blackburn, Holloway was sent to the stand after some heated exchanges with the visiting dug-out and an assistant referee.

Ollie even told the lino, 'Santa's coming and you won't be getting any presents for Christmas.' He must have done some serious damage to the eardrums of fourth officials.

The gaffer stressed to his players not to become involved and then did the opposite. He was full of remorse when he had cooled down, but his actions merely underlined his passion for the game and how desperate and determined he was to win every single match.

I share those emotions and when my will to win has spilled over I had fallen foul of the authorities. For that I have regrets, though I cannot apologise for my actions.

IAN HOLLOWAY moved me from right-back to centre-half towards the end of 2013/14 and after just a dozen games in my new role I felt I was a better central defender than I had been a full-back.

As a right-back I always did enough to get by, reliable defensively, but not as effective going forward. I was never one to run with the ball and cross it as modern full-backs have to.

In the middle of the defence, you do not need to be outstanding at taking the ball into the opponents' half because that is not your job. You just need to be a solid, dependable defender and that was something the gaffer saw in me. With my passing a strong point, Ollie thought he could nurture me into becoming a top-class central defender.

Listening to Holloway as he taught me what I needed to know to make the switch, the change proved much easier than I had anticipated. It almost came naturally to me and I was enjoying my football more than ever before.

I've always loved defending, heading and kicking the ball, and I regret I did not change positions earlier in my career. No manager had ever been able to persuade me or give me the confidence that I could do it before Holloway.

His man-management skills were exceptional. Some managers are only concerned with those in the first-team squad, but Ollie would go out of his way to do all he could to improve the fringe players, to help them move up the pecking order.

He made time for the underage teams, he loved to chat to the groundsman, the kitchen staff, everyone. He did all he could to make every single person working for Millwall feel part of the club.

Ollie treated everybody with the same respect because to him if you worked for Millwall you must be special.

✻ ✻ ✻ ✻ ✻

WHEN IAN HOLLOWAY joined Millwall one of his first tasks was to cut out the moaning. If a club is doing badly, as we were for much of 2013/14, players tend to highlight negatives; the food, training, the pitch, the kit, the football…you name it, someone would bitch about it. I think some players need a good moan to get them through the day – including myself.

The gaffer made it a priority to eliminate this, not least the body language of a player throwing his arms in the air if a team-mate's pass was poor either in training or during matches. This sends out all the wrong signals.

I remember The Hof (Stefan Maierhofer) was absolutely slaughtered after one game because of this – Ollie thought it sent out all the wrong messages which fed fuel to the crowd.

It took Holloway a while to make everyone realise that a whinge achieved nothing except to create bad vibes. He spent much of his first month on this and while there will always be something for somebody to complain about, this should be justified and not just done for the sake of having a gripe.

Unfortunately, the dressing-room disharmony Holloway had worked hard at to improve returned in 2014/15 as the fight against the drop intensified.

✻ ✻ ✻ ✻ ✻

ONE THING Ian Holloway would not tolerate is lateness. He never accepted any excuse; roadworks, traffic jam, bad weather, dodgy alarm clock…his standard response was, 'Leave earlier, just in case.'

The gaffer regarded lateness so badly he compared it to someone shitting on his nan's doorstep and walking off.

Ricardo Fuller was a few minutes late for a home game against Blackpool – Millwall players had to report by 1.15pm – because he was in the car park signing autographs. The manager called David Forde and I into his office and said, 'I want to drop him. What do you think?'

I said, 'Gaffer, we have worked all week on a system that includes Ricardo. Maybe give him the benefit of the doubt on this occasion. If it happens again, drop him.'

The manager returned to the changing room and said to Fuller, 'You are lucky. These two lads here have kept you in the team. I was going to leave you out.'

Holloway was so passionate about football that turning up even a minute late was a cardinal sin. He believed that if you are running late in your car you became anxious which can affect your preparation for the game.

Fuller played, but was still fined for being late, which probably made the autographs among the most expensive he had ever signed.

He is possibly the most fined professional I've known. He either has too much money or is living in Jamaican time.

If we were ever late for a home game a second time it cost us between £500 and £1,500 based on previous offences.

Yup, best to leave earlier.

17

Beaten by an 'Olympic' sprinter

Because he had a false start

THE MODERN-DAY footballer is becoming faster, stronger and more powerful. Fitness and recovery are crucial in order for players to be at the top of their game on a consistent basis. Arsène Wenger was one of the first to demonstrate his philosophy, introducing key areas of diet and nutrition as well as fitness regimes designed to produce better results.

A significant difference to some previous managers I had worked with whose culture was of the old school run, run, run until you drop with beans on toast for a pre-match meal.

Pre-seasons are now less of the dreaded cross-country lung-busters, the emphasis on more structured three-minute runs with sprint techniques, yoyo and bleep tests. This technique has also filtered through to the lower leagues. The technology available means those clubs can compete with the best within their budget.

At Millwall, fitness was constantly monitored, with players' body fat, which had to be less than 12 per cent, checked on a monthly basis, though the goalkeepers were given a little more leeway. Luckily for me I have never had an issue with my weight. Some are less fortunate and were put on a strict diet programme.

Every player dreaded body fat day as being over the 12 per cent mark meant they were in the red zone and this could affect a manager's thinking because if there is any sign of a drop in performance the issue of your body fat and lifestyle was immediately questioned.

Some only have to look at a jam doughnut to put on weight.

Fortunately for me, but annoyingly for others including my wife, I can eat just about anything and my weight remains stable at 73 or 74kg.

✻ ✻ ✻ ✻ ✻

A PLAYER'S diet tends to improve as he becomes older because experience teaches him what he needs to do. I have two meals a day at the training ground, normally four days a week, with porridge followed by eggs on toast for breakfast washed down by a black coffee or green tea. I also take supplements such as creatine, proteins, vitamins and cod liver oil. After training it is usually fish or chicken with potatoes, rice and salad.

As a family we like to eat out quite often for dinner because I relish the variety of food that restaurants can offer. And I don't have to load the dishwasher after. In fact, I am almost obsessed with food. Eating is not something that should be done just to satisfy your hunger, it should also be enjoyed for its quality.

Sunday is what we call our cheat day, our day of indulgence. If we've won or the missus is in a good mood it will be a Full Monty breakfast – wonderful – with the occasional takeaway, mainly a Chinese, in the evening. My guilty pleasure is that I like to have a small glass of red wine some nights with my dinner. Ray Wilkins used to let the senior Millwall players have a glass of red with their meal on away games on a Friday. This goes back to his days with AC Milan and he said it was a ritual in Italy.

IF I HAD not been a footballer I think I would have become a chef or joined the Marines – very different lifestyles. I would have loved to have worked in a top restaurant, preparing the best food. My dad was in the Navy and, when I was growing up, he told me so many stories of how he saw the world.

A couple of years ago, Aimee and I were in the New Forest at our favourite restaurant, the Michelin-starred Chewton Glen which was voted the number one holiday hotel in the UK. We were married in the hotel so it is very close to our hearts and our meal, as usual, was ten out of ten. Not only is the food excellent, their wine list is one of the largest in the UK.

Imagine my delight when the maître d' told me there was a Millwall fan who worked in the kitchen – he had spotted me and wanted to say hello. However, he was not allowed to go in to the restaurant area because his head and arms were covered in tattoos.

I was invited into the kitchen to meet him. He was so pleased to see me and it was humbling to meet a fellow Lion with such enthusiasm for Millwall.

I was also thrilled to be shown around and meet the guys who had prepared our dinner which was beautifully cooked and presented.

* * * * *

FITNESS IN FOOTBALL is all-important and clubs now have the use of GPS trackers along with heart-rate monitors as players' everyday fitness is checked. These can detect in training what distance and how fast players run, how many short sprints they do and what rate their heart reaches. This is designed to calculate how hard players are training or what workload they are enduring plus, of course, if anyone is only pretending to work which some have tried over the years.

By having this technology available and using these specific running tests there is no hiding place. With speed tests I could hold my own with the fastest at Millwall.

However, I had no idea that on one occasion I would have to prove myself against an Olympic-trained team-mate.

* * * * *

DENNIS WISE liked to introduce different aspects to training to ensure things didn't become too regimented. One morning I arrived to find Wisey, Kevin Muscat and others arguing about which player at the club was the quickest.

The two candidates for the Millwall Sprint Championship were myself and Mark McCammon.

An in-house bookmakers had been opened on who would win the 100m dash, with Wisey saying to me, 'You are the favourite, my money's on you Dunney, don't let me down.'

McCammon had undergone sprint training with Dwain Chambers, the fourth fastest Briton to run the 100m and who had competed at the Olympic Games and World Championships. I thought I was going to take part in a training session, suddenly I am racing a guy who had enjoyed professional guidance from one of Britain's best ever sprinters while the manager had a few quid on me beating him. No pressure then.

There were eight players in the 100m race, the other six doing little more than making up the numbers. Wisey had put poles up as makeshift starting and finishing lines. I had never been so nervous in my life. I knew I was quick, but I also knew McCammon was a powerhouse.

On your marks…get set…and the start whistle was blown. I am convinced McCammon went a split second early so he had the initial advantage, but I caught him up and we were neck and neck for virtually the entire race. We crossed the finishing line as near as damn it together. McCammon continued running with a victorious arm in the air, probably attempting some athletics mind games.

A photo-finish, if you can have such a thing without a photo. A not particularly neutral panel of so-called judges, including Wisey, who understandably ruled that I had won, decided the winner. The manager was outnumbered and McCammon was declared the winner.

Mark is now a fitness instructor at Herbalife. His nickname was 'Hightower' after the character in *Police Academy*.

But had he not got off to such a dubious start I would have had him.

18

Snorers, plate-lickers and the Beckham from Peckham's unusual night ritual

My weird and wonderful Millwall team-mates

SOMETHING I have always struggled with, and it is as important as diet and fitness, is sleep, which is vital for recovery. I have to be one of the worst sleepers. Any noise, even the sound of rain or a clock ticking, any movement and I cannot sleep a wink.

Night games are the worst as we take in so much caffeine and sugary drinks which, along with the adrenalin of the match, keep me awake for hours.

149

Having roomed at Millwall with David Forde for many years there were countless times his snoring would ensure almost zero kip for me. Fordey and I occasionally shared a room with two single beds, but some were so close that if he rolled over we would be spooning.

Not good. Not good at all.

I had also roomed with Kevin Braniff and Peter Sweeney for most of my early years with the Lions, fun times they were. Sweeney became so angry when losing on the PlayStation he would rip curtains off the walls, bite remote controls or punch lampshades and doors.

He probably took it just a little bit too seriously.

The worst room-mate to share with was James Henry. He has a snoring issue so bad you had to check he had not swallowed a sock. I shared a room with him on one away trip and was forced to go down to reception at 3am and beg the hotel to give me another room. 'Whatever the cost is I'll pay it, just get me out of here.'

Luckily the hotel found me a single room and did not charge me for it. That was the last time me or anyone ever shared a room with snoring king Henry.

Most players shared rooms because Millwall thought it was an ideal way to bond as being stuck in a room on your own can be pretty boring. For the older players who had kids, spending time on our own on away trips could be absolutely magical. While we loved our children, we also loved the occasional night of peace and quiet. Snorers permitting.

Rooms were normally shared with someone who played in your position, such as defenders together, midfielders, strikers and so forth. The most difficult to share with were the new players who had signed on a Friday which meant there had been no time to speak, but you then were thrown into a room together.

If neither knew each other conversation could be awkward, especially if they did not speak good English.

* * * * *

WHEN IT comes to food, I am one of the fussiest eaters you will ever meet. Chefs and dinner ladies over the years can vouch for that as I have driven them all mad since I started full-time aged 15.

Fordey is another player who, like me, can moan about food, but his plate was always spotless. He licked his plate clean – literally. Baffled me, that one.

As for professionalism, fitness and diet Darren Ward was in a league – or a world – of his own, you decide.

Ward was nicknamed the 'Beckham from Peckham', but I doubt whether David from Leytonstone used to set his alarm during the night so he could brush his teeth and sometimes even perform sit-ups and press-ups.

Someone who was rooming with Ward told me this. I was never sure if he was joking. Probably not.

Ward is the most diet- and health-conscious player I have known. He never put anything in his body unless he had examined the contents. When we had a team night out, he would bring a banana and some nuts to eat with his gin and tonic (two or three G&Ts were his maximum). This was to counteract any alcohol going into his liver.

He never drank tap water or regular bottled water; instead he had his own favourite brand which was designed not to bloat you during performance. His toothpaste was hand-picked because he wanted no chemicals or additives. When he was massaged he insisted on his own oil to be used on his body. He wore something on his wrist to counter the sun's emissions.

Millwall's pre-match meal on away games would be the usual chicken, potatoes, pasta or rice, but Ward would bring his own food which was organic chicken or vegetables steam-cooked or quinoa. No gluten whatsoever. His breakfast would be nuts, berries, seeds, pineapple etc.

Ward would not use table salt, only sea salt. Ketchup or any sauces were no-go areas. He bought his own protein as opposed to that which the club supplied, which must have cost him a fortune.

He was obsessed with taking and doing the right things to the extent I think it affected his football. For me, he almost became more interested in his preparation than the actual game.

Ward was an elite professional in a different way and a lot of players learned from his approach. He was his own individual and I respected him for that.

He said the lifespan of a human should be 120, but how long we are around is dictated by how we live our lives.

✳   ✳   ✳   ✳   ✳

IT WAS A Millwall tradition that when a player joined the club, on his first away trip he had to sing a song in front of the entire squad, even if the idea was a little dated, not least because young players have much better voices than their predecessors. I chose a song by Hearsay. As I stood up before an audience just waiting to give me grief, I had stage-fright and could barely open my mouth. These days the new boys are full of confidence and sing like they should be on *The X Factor*.

They receive shouts for an encore they are so good, but Chris Wood did something different. Very different.

As a New Zealander, Wood inevitably loves rugby and he treated his Millwall team-mates to a one-man version of the Haka which is a highlight of any game involving the All Blacks. He was brilliant, doing all the arm, head and tongue movements complete with the jump at the end.

He was so realistic a few of the boys were a little scared.

I was fascinated because it was so unusual, an unexpected pleasure from Wood, who is a humble, unassuming guy, a lovely lad. It was a huge surprise for a relatively quiet person to perform one of sport's most memorable and intimidating rituals.

Kenny Jackett, who, like the rest of us, could hardly believe what he had seen, was also impressed. Whether Wood's inspirational introduction to the squad had anything to do with this I don't know, but Millwall went on a 13-game unbeaten run with the Kiwi dominant, scoring 11 goals in 19 matches.

His hold-up play was among the best I've seen. David Forde could hit the ball anywhere near Wood who, helped by his big, broad shoulders, would control it on his chest before laying it off.

I knew about Wood before he joined Millwall on loan from West Bromwich Albion in 2012, not least because he had scored against us.

But until he arrived at The Den I was not aware of just how good a striker he was. Jackett got the best out of Wood, helping him realise the potential he had shown while on previous loans to Barnsley, Brighton, Birmingham City and Bristol City.

Millwall could have afforded the reported fee of £2m to make Wood's transfer permanent and my understanding was that the club offered him more money than Leicester did. He decided he wanted to be nearer his house in the Midlands while the Thai-based consortium who had taken over at Leicester were promising to spend big money to reach the Premier League, which they did in 2014.

As much as I would have loved Wood to stay, I can understand why he chose Leicester, but in many ways Millwall were responsible for his big pay-day.

* * * * *

EVERY PLAYER has his own pre-match ritual. Mine has always started before I leave my house, be it for a home game or an away trip, and is always the same.

For home games, just before I leave my house I like to bless myself with holy water from Lourdes, a sanctuary in France which is one of the world's leading Catholic shrines where the spring water is believed to possess healing qualities.

My mum loved the place, so it reminds me of her. I feel she watches over me when I play, so holy water makes me feel safe.

If I failed to do this – and I never have – I know it would affect my preparations for the game. Crazy some may think, but there are rituals all footballers have to hide their pre-match nerves.

As I wore the number two jersey at Millwall I liked to be second on the pitch, though that was before I was made captain in August 2014. I always put Vicks on my chest, whether it's summer or winter. I'm not really sure why, it's just something I have done ever since I was a kid, so why change now?

I have my legs massaged with oil and hot rub, which helps with slide tackles and grass burns. I have worn studs throughout my career and to the surprise of many even during pre-season when most players prefer moulds as the pitches are so hard. It is something I was told to do as a young defender and I have continued to do this.

Some Millwall players' rituals were more unusual. For example, Robbie Ryan urinated in a certain toilet, always on the right, wherever he went.

Matt Lawrence insisted his jersey, shorts, socks and boots were laid out immaculately with everything in a particular place. The kit man did such a great job not even an Army sergeant major could criticise his work.

Some players went into their own world, listening to whatever music helped them prepare for the match. Lewis Grabban was one who prayed while others used a certain tape round their wrist or wore lucky shin pads which they never changed.

A lot of it is in the mind, of course, but it's whatever makes you feel comfortable before you go out to battle.

Stuart Nethercott used to make himself throw up before every game. We could hear him roaring in the toilet as he made himself sick. He would then wash his face and be ready to go to war. As a young lad I admit I found this a bit scary.

WHILE I have had no serious injuries, I was fortunate to make it to 30 after goalkeeper Graham Stack was involved in an accident in the world's fastest truck.

It was after a pre-season friendly at Southend – the players made their own way to and from such matches.

Stack had a friend who allowed him to try out different cars and for the game at Roots Hall he turned up in a Viper-powered Dodge Ram truck which had a 6.7-litre engine, 0–60 in five seconds.

It was in the *Guinness Book of Records* as the world's fastest production truck.

I was the passenger on the way to the game, but luckily for me Joe Dolan drove us home because he lived nearer me while Stack was based in west London.

On the journey home Dolan and I were behind Stacky and as he passed through a roundabout on the outskirts of Southend, it appeared that he floored it. The truck wobbled, skidded and spun into a barrier before hitting the wall of, ironically, a car showroom. A wheel came off and went flying down the road.

I could see smoke coming out of the engine with green liquid leaking from it. I was certain the truck was going to blow up.

We pulled over and my immediate thought was to get him out of the vehicle. He was barely conscious, but Dolan and I could not open the driver's door. We raced round the truck and dragged him out which was not easy given the damage to the passenger side. He stumbled to a safe area, we called the police and the ambulance service who took him to hospital. The air bag probably saved Stack's life, but had I been a passenger I doubt whether I would be here today. The passenger side was demolished, just about everything was crushed.

I cannot see how I would have survived. There but for the grace of God.

We went to hospital with Stack and Pamela, Neil Harris's mum who lived nearby, brought us some tea and coffee. Stacky was not injured, just traumatised and was kept in overnight – Dolan and I were also in shock after witnessing what happened, but Joe was OK to complete the journey home.

Stack seemingly underestimated the power of the vehicle when he accelerated and the truck was a write-off. Word was Stacky's mate was not best pleased.

MARC BIRCHAM, who was a Millwall player between 1996 and 2002, told a story about a snake when he was away playing for Canada.

The kit man hated snakes so for a laugh the players went to a local pet shop and bought one, thinking it would be fun to put it in his bath. It then occurred to them that snakes need heat, so it was taken out of the bath and put on the floor, Birch filling up the bath with hot water to keep the snake happy.

When the kit man returned, he went to the bathroom where a combination of seeing the snake and the heat coming from the water caused him to faint. Thankfully, he was okay.

IT WASN'T a snake that made me faint...it was a Treasure Chest.

Myself, David Forde and Richard Chaplow took our wives to the West End. After dinner, we went to Mahiki's where we ordered their famous Treasure Chest – far from being full of valuable coins or what have you, it contains champagne and goodness knows how many cocktails which we all drank through long straws.

Whenever I have a drink I always fall asleep in the car going home. I woke up when we arrived at our house, climbed out of the taxi and fainted, the situation not helped by the fact I had my hands in my coat pocket so could not break my fall.

By this time, Fordey was on the other side of the road and all he could see was me with my face in the kerb. He thought it was amusing until he saw the state of me. My head and face were cut to the extent an ambulance was called and I was taken to hospital where they repaired the wounds the best they could.

The following day I had to report for a Junior Lions party. It was a cold day so I pulled down my bobble hat as much as I could to cover the cuts, but my bloody secret was soon revealed. Steve Lomas, the manager at the time, found it amusing and thought I'd been involved in a fight.

'I hope the other geezer looks worse,' he said.

I told him that I had fainted when I got out of the car, but he wouldn't believe me.

* * * * *

AT MILLWALL all the players were involved with a lot of charity work and visiting local schools. It was in our contracts, but I would have done it regardless because it gives something back to the community.

To see the faces of kids who are in hospital when footballers come to meet them is priceless. At schools we did question-and-answer sessions, though the questions were as much about which car we drove, how much we earned or what sort of phone we had as our greatest game or hardest opponent.

Millwall take part in a lot of community work and if I, as ambassador for the club, had to give up a couple of hours every two weeks to visit hospitals and schools it was a most enjoyable 'chore'.

It is great fun to talk to kids and try to help them improve their football.

I have been involved with the local Demelza Hospice for sick children. The hospice helps kids up to the age of 19 who are not expected to reach adulthood because of degenerative conditions.

To see young boys and girls who will never experience the full joy of life is heartbreaking and I was happy to give some time and be part of a fundraising quiz night when I could.

✳ ✳ ✳ ✳ ✳

OVER THE last 24 years I have played with hundreds of different team-mates from all over the world. Some were exceptional players, great lads who have given me wonderful memories and laughs along the way. Like any job, I have also met clowns, some who rate themselves highly and think they are better than the club. Many have been there to pick up their wages and could not care less what the result is come Saturday.

These players, who really get to me, were the ones I call spoofers, the bullshitters who go through each week hoping no one would notice them blagging their way through a game or hiding in training, gym work or running sessions.

There will always be big-ego players and many with personal agendas, but this is just part of football, not exclusive to any single club. Those who are not playing or who are in and out of the side can be an issue in the dressing room. They can try to disrupt the team by causing friction and negative energy among the squad. These lads are poison.

Thankfully, most players are good honest pros with exceptional banter who give their all for the cause. These are the guys you need when times get tough.

I have always doubted whether loan players can give as much to a club as those on permanent contracts.

Players who come in on loan, especially from Premier League teams, are usually on more money than those in the Championship or League 1 and have stepped down a level in order to get some playing time.

I can understand this to a certain extent because they are not really attached to the club they are spending just a few weeks or months with. Young players are usually grateful for the chance to play regularly and will try their best to show their parent club they are ready for more regular first-team football when they return.

However, older players who, for whatever reason, are out of favour with their parent club, do not always have the same commitment.

Andros Townsend, Harry Kane, Ryan Fredericks and Ryan Mason, in fact, all the young Tottenham lads loaned to Millwall, were terrific, so was Arsenal's Benik Afobe. If they proved they could play for Millwall, which they did, they can play anywhere.

I think you have to ensure you do not have too many loan players at any given time because this can create a problem. Watford had 14 in 2012/13, ten from Udinese, though the Football League changed its rules and now only five players loaned from overseas can be named in matchday squads, with just four from a single club.

We were told that Jose Mourinho would not let any of his young boys join Millwall because we had too many senior players. His belief, apparently, was that too many older players could affect the lads' confidence by being bullish.

Or maybe it was just Millwall.

A club can bring in a maximum of eight players throughout the course of a season which can be a double-edged sword.

Some sides have won promotion with loan players a crucial part of their success, but when they go up they have to be replaced.

19

Football's mind games can work

Zaha almost disappeared after we had words

CRICKET HAS its sledging and football has its mind games. I became very good at what I was taught about intimidating other players, especially the big-name stars. The right words at the right time to an opponent can have the desired effect. The sentiments are not meant in a literal way. They are just jagged-edged banter.

I learned a lot from Dennis Wise and Kevin Muscat about how to wind up opponents, though given that they accumulated 25 red cards between them during their playing days there may be some raised eyebrows at my choice of mentors.

Muscat, who was also a full-back, was a close friend. He had made a good career for himself, having played for Rangers where he helped them win the Treble in 2002/03 and was financially very well off.

He also allowed me to drive his Porsche 911 Turbo – a dream car – occasionally.

* * * * *

IN 2013, Millwall played Crystal Palace at The Den and Ian Holloway was in charge of the visitors. Within two minutes I told Wilfried Zaha, who was later to join Manchester United for around £15m, with a smile, 'I hope your first touch is fucking good because your second touch, I will break you in half.'

He smiled back and laughed, but after our first coming-together he knew I wasn't joking. I hardly saw him the rest of the game.

I was asked in an interview before the match about whether he was worth the valuation of £20m Palace had put on him and I said it was a ridiculous amount for any Championship player. As Palace had valued him at £20m it was obvious they would accept the £15m United eventually offered.

My view brought me a lot of abuse on social media from Palace fans who even made up a song about me which they sung at every home and away game for the remainder of the season. Let's just say it wasn't flattering.

Zak Whitbread, who was at Leicester at the time, told me he couldn't believe the visiting Palace fans were singing a silly song about me.

While Palace supporters were upset with what I had said, they now know I was correct. It was great business for the club and Zaha returned to Selhurst Park on loan in 2014/15 so they benefited to the tune of a possible £15m and got their star winger back.

I think Zaha is a good player with the potential to play regularly at the highest level as he is proving at Palace after signing a permanent deal, but I am still awaiting my first apology from any of their fans.

✳ ✳ ✳ ✳ ✳

ALSO in 2013, when Millwall played against Leicester, I had words with Lloyd Dyer, a former team-mate whose electric pace and power frightened me.

'Don't start running at me with the ball because I'll put you in Row Z,' I said, again with a smile.

He replied, 'I'm not falling for that, Dunney, I'm not a young kid any more.'

I gave him the look to show him I wasn't bluffing.

Following our initial challenge, I went for him knowing I'd miss him. It was just to make sure he could feel me breathing down his neck and to mess with his head.

I never saw him again throughout the game. My mind games worked because Dyer kept telling one of our players that I was crazy and I would be sent off. He might be correct about the crazy bit, but I wasn't dismissed.

As an old-school full-back I had to use these tools, though full-backs do so much attacking now they are almost wingers. Defenders have not been brought up like we were in our youth teams. Full-backs like I was are slowly moving out of the modern game.

During some games, in the heat of the moment, I have had a split second in which to make a decision. I never set out with a premeditated agenda to deliberately hurt opponents involved in any of my red cards, bookings or controversies.

Michael Doyle of Coventry City came as close as anyone to being an exception.

For some reason, when the Sky Blues beat us 2-1 in the FA Cup in January 2008, Doyle wouldn't leave me alone during the match. He elbowed me, kicked me, pinched me; I had no idea what the hell his problem was, but something about me was irritating him. Maybe he knew I was hot-headed and was trying to play his own mind games to get me sent off.

After 32 minutes there was a drop ball and it happened that Doyle and I were the players contesting possession. This was my chance.

Jackpot. Doyle was first to the ball and I caught him full weight behind me on his shin. He was on the floor for about five or six minutes receiving treatment.

Yes, I wanted to send a message to him because he had been almost bullying me for half an hour. I certainly wouldn't advise anyone to do the same and go for the ball in such an aggressive manner, but sometimes in life you have to stick up for yourself.

I do, occasionally, have a nasty streak in me. It's who I am. The chances are if I didn't do what I did to an opponent, then it would happen to me. And it has.

Nathan Ellington, who played for Wigan, Watford, Derby and Ipswich among others, left me needing eight stitches in my forehead after he caught me with his elbow. I have no idea if he did it deliberately, though I felt he knew what he was doing. However, the referee took no action against him.

Marian Pahars of Southampton broke my cheekbone as we jumped for the ball following a throw-in during a game in April 2006. Again, it was an elbow that did the damage, leaving me with the worst pain I have ever experienced. It was the day Millwall were relegated to League 1 and Pahars was playing left-midfield in front of a young left-back called Gareth Bale, making his Saints debut.

After Pahars caught me, I could feel a bone pressing out of my cheek below my right eye. I'm not one to go down for no reason and the Millwall physio knew straight away it was bad, so I was substituted immediately to receive medical attention.

I was examined by a doctor who told me I would have to go to hospital. I showered, dressed and climbed on to the coach distraught about being relegated while my face was in agony. Despite being hungry I could not eat, I was only allowed to take water or fruit juice through a straw – my mood not helped by the lads offering me wine gums. It was not the best journey home I have experienced.

Back at The Den, the physio drove me to King's College Hospital where I underwent surgery. A piece of bone was taken from my hip and placed in my cheek. I stayed in hospital overnight and went home the following day, complete with mask to protect the fracture – one of three bones I'd had broken in my career.

An accident? Only the player making the challenge knows.

20

Beware of smooth-talking agents

Many have just their own interests at heart

EW IN football are above agents in the unpopularity stakes. I was fortunate, but I would warn young players to take advice from senior professionals before choosing their agent.

My first agent was John Mac. Dave Livermore recommended him to me while I was still a Millwall YTS and my initial reaction as a 17-year-old was that I must be doing all right for him to think I needed an agent. I was flattered.

Agents like to sign young hopefuls because sometimes it can be easy money for them. If a young player doesn't get a pro contract, so what? They cost the agent nothing, but if they do, the agent is paid very well for basically a couple of one-hour meetings at the max.

A player signs his first pro contract and starts earning, let's say, a standard £350 to £500 a week. Your previous contract was £45 a week. All the hard work has been done by yourself to get to pro level, but you are now made to believe your agent is responsible for the rise.

You start to think he is the bee's knees. The player is now hooked and signs another two-year contract with the agent. It goes on and on until the player is released or has no more interest from anywhere.

It is then you start to see who your agent really is.

The money agents can make from contracts or transfers can be tens of thousands up to millions for the top end of the scale. This is why it can be such a ruthless business in the agents' and players' market.

Livermore, who is well respected at Millwall, introduced me to John, who also represented my team-mate Joe Dolan. I felt that because they were good, honest lads this would be reflected in their agent. I think I made the right choice. John Mac was a very experienced agent who I believed would be good for me when I needed him.

I signed a two-year deal with John and he negotiated my first contract with Millwall. His payment would have been along the lines of three to five per cent of the overall deal.

I was offered £350 a week for my first year, £450 for year two and £500 for year three with a £6,000 signing-on fee spread over the three years. That was substantial money for a kid from a council estate with little or no outgoings. I was buzzing.

John seemed to understand this teenage street kid hoping to make his mark with Millwall and we got on really well. He'd been there, seen it, done it and he knew the game. I respected his experience and words of wisdom. We had a good relationship and though many see agents as little more than a necessary evil, as a young lad I could not possibly have negotiated my own contract with the club.

I was not educated in the world of financial dealings, not confident enough to speak to the manager, chief executive and chairman about such things. I was happy with the deals John arranged for me – he finalised the contract and then negotiated his fee with the club.

What I now know is that most agents' fees come out of the player's contract. For example, if the two-year contract is worth £500,000 his fee, probably five per cent (£25,000) comes out of this, so the player's deal is only £475,000.

Although you think the club is paying him, it is really you. And if the club does pay your agent, you can still be liable for the tax on it. Players should be very careful when signing with an agent and letting him negotiate for them.

John Mac became a friend who gave me a lot of good advice. I remember when things were not going well for me at Millwall and instead of saying I should consider a transfer, which many agents would because it is more lucrative for them, he said I should remain at The Den and hopefully become a respected one-club man.

By staying with Millwall until 2015 it meant I had never had the significant increase in wages that comes with a move, though I was given a testimonial by the club. A one-club player will invariably be among the lower earners but you cannot put a price on being loyal to one club, especially one you love.

I'd always been happy at Millwall and while I may have had a few more quid in the bank, I have no regrets about staying at The Den for 23 years.

I am very grateful for what I have and as you get older you realise that money doesn't always buy you happiness.

With a few years' experience behind me, I negotiated my last two Millwall contracts myself, more confident and worldly-wise at 28 than I was at 17. This was more beneficial to me, but it was difficult telling John I did not need him any longer. We remain friends and he is still there for me should I need him.

Kenny Jackett told me the experience of negotiating my own contract would help me if I wanted to go down the road of being a manager.

I sat down with Jackett and chief executive Andy Ambler and the contract was agreed with few problems.

✳　✳　✳　✳　✳

WHILE I HAD no complaints about John Mac, many players are not so fortunate with their representatives. Some agents can sell themselves superbly, taking a young player for a meal at a top hotel and telling him the sort of money he could make, assuring him that other players he represents are on similar salaries, promising him help with buying a house and arranging a mortgage.

It is easy to be sucked in by such smooth talking and players fall for it because they know no better.

A lot of agents are trained to tell you what you want to hear.

Apart from unscrupulous agents, players also have to be wary of financial advisers who normally come with the agent and who know 'guaranteed' ways of making big bucks very quickly. There are too many corrupt people just waiting to get their hands on players' money and who do not have their best interests at heart.

Only their own.

We hear far too many stories about footballers going bankrupt. They have invested in tax schemes, image rights, overseas property and accounts, even in film schemes, all promising huge rewards. Some got lucky and have made money.

But over the last five years the government have closed financial loopholes leaving many liable for tax bills they never thought they would have and cannot pay.

As soon as you sign a deal, some agents try to talk you into joining a pension scheme or an insurance agreement, which you are assured are good, safe, solid investments. Yet so many footballers have lost money on various dodgy deals that they were assured was like printing money.

It can be difficult to trust too many people in that world because they are only out for themselves.

Clubs do not do enough for players in this respect. Each club should have some sort of independent financial adviser to look after players' mortgages, pensions and investments, someone whose priority is not to line his or her own pockets.

Apprentices and young professionals have little idea of the ins and outs of mortgages or car agreements or even how to get a credit card. At the age of 18, you suddenly have more money than ever and you need help. A friend of a friend can tell a young player about some property scheme in the Bahamas that is guaranteed to double his money in five years and it is easy to be attracted by such sweet talk.

Even top internationals who are millionaires lose money on so-called nailed-on investments.

If clubs employed a specialist financial expert to educate players and help them with any early investments it would hopefully mean fewer quick profits for the sharks. They should explain to YTS players, particularly, that if a deal seems too good to be true it probably will be.

Players should not have to learn the hard way, there should be more awareness of finances when they climb on the football ladder.

One day you are earning very little, then you sign a pro contract and suddenly you are rich in comparison. It can be easy to be drawn into a potentially dangerous world of investments and it is important young players are given early help and advice.

I have been close to putting money into overseas property deals including one in Morocco where I sent a deposit to secure what I thought was a lucrative investment. At the last minute I cancelled the cheque as Aimee said that putting money in an overseas development where you do not speak the language was not the best idea.

The agents put on a professional display to sell their products, which are impressive. From ski resorts in France to property in the Caribbean, they come to you and the only guarantee is that they will make quick money out of your investments.

Players whose teams have been promoted can be particularly vulnerable. Success means a nice bonus, ready cash which is ripe for the agents' various schemes.

Like vultures the money-men are waiting to feast.

The business deals may be legal, but nowhere near the 'wonderful investments' that the agents try to convince you that they are. Not too long ago the Spanish property market was the next big thing – now, people who bought houses or apartments are struggling to sell them for half of what they paid.

Former Aston Villa midfielder Lee Hendrie is just one who lost all his money and was declared bankrupt in 2012. Jermaine Wright, a former team-mate who went on to join Southampton, is one who lost money on schemes and property abroad.

I have heard hundreds of similar stories from wealthy footballers over the years who were worse off because of such investments.

The best place for your money is probably in the bank. Interest rates may be low, but I am not an overseas property expert or stocks and shares gambler.

I would rather know my money is safe than risk the sort of losses I hear too much about.

✳ ✳ ✳ ✳ ✳

THE TOP agents, like Jorge Mendes and Pini Zahavi, are probably richer than most of the players they represent. Mendes's Gestifute agency includes José Mourinho, Cristiano Ronaldo, Nani, Anderson, Pepe, Ricardo Carvalho, Raul Meireles, Radamel Falcao and Fábio Coentrão.

When Manchester United published their 2004 accounts they showed that the payment to agents on the Ronaldo deal to Real Madrid had been £1.129m. That was loose change compared with the £30m Neymar's father received when his son joined Barcelona from Santos, by far the biggest commission ever paid in football.

FIFA statistics showed that 28 per cent of transfer fees – almost a third – go to agents and third parties. UEFA claimed agent fees represent the average equivalent of an extra 12.6 per cent of the transfer fee.

Some Premier League clubs pay £15m to agents each season. That is the total of all 24 clubs in the Championship.

There are 24 registered agents in China, where football is booming, who can earn £1.5m a year each.

While my contracts have been fairly straightforward, some Premier League players can have several lucrative clauses in their agreements. For example, a loyalty bonus for seeing out his contract at a club and it will be paid on the last game of the season in the final year of a contract.

Some have appearance money in their deals. A player could get 100 per cent of this for a start, maybe 50 per cent for coming on as a substitute and 25 per cent as a non-playing sub. There can also be bonuses paid if a team wins the league, a cup, qualifies for Europe or makes a certain round of the cup. Maybe goalscoring bonuses, a clean sheet bonus, international bonuses and award bonuses.

Former agent Peter Harrison admitted he took advantage of the naivety of ex-West Ham chairman Eggert Magnusson to pocket £900,000 in commission in the deal to sign former Millwall defender Lucas Neill. Harrison said, 'The commission with the club is whatever you can negotiate. When I took Lucas Neill to West Ham instead of Liverpool I earned £900,000 and they put the player on £72,000 a week.'

I was told a 17-year-old at a Premier League club was recently paid £100,000 to sign with an agency despite not yet making a competitive first-team appearance.

Nice work if you can get it.

21

Wise's broken FA Cup Final promise

For a few seconds, I was George Best

DENNIS WISE was selfish and probably unprofessional to play in the 2004 FA Cup Final against Manchester United. But I don't blame him.

The Millwall player-manager was not fully fit because of a calf injury, which was almost certain to rule him out of the game. He had flown to Italy for last-chance treatment during the build-up. Taking into account his previous FA Cup achievements and the fact this was to be his fourth final in the competition, I would have done the same.

Do I hold it against Wise that he selected himself and therefore I had to miss out? No.

My biggest problem was the promise that I would play some part in the game. I was assured that Wise would play only the first 20 minutes and then I would come on as a substitute.

The nearest I came to playing at the Millennium Stadium was warming up.

I would have loved to have come on, even for one minute, but Wise chose to give Curtis Weston his 15 minutes of fame instead. At 17 years and 119 days, Weston became the youngest player to appear in the FA Cup Final. Wise was aware of this and good luck to Weston, a smashing lad, but it hurt me that I never got on. As we were losing 3-0 and it was the last minute maybe there was no reason to bring me on. The match was effectively over. But it is something I shall never forget.

While disappointed, which is putting it mildly, as a young player just making my way into the team I had no right to confront the manager. This is part of the business we are in. Wise remains a friend, though I have never brought the subject up with him, possibly out of respect.

One day I may ask him to explain his decision not to bring me on.

What has happened cannot be changed. In football, as in life, you have highs and lows, but I would still like to hear why he chose to bring on Weston rather than me.

* * * * *

DESPITE THE loss, the occasion gave me a drive, an ambition to achieve something similar in football again, either playing or managing. The build-up, the banter and being the focus of media attention was an education. It was where I wanted to be. The experience made me stronger as a person. I'd had a taste of the big time and I wanted more.

I was there as a Millwall player and a Millwall fan. They are memories that will stay with me forever.

Even if you win only one cap for your country, perhaps as a substitute, it can never be taken away from you. And coming on to play one minute of an FA Cup Final, especially against Manchester United, could never have been taken away from me.

It wasn't meant to be, it wasn't my day.

✳　✳　✳　✳　✳

ON THE Tuesday before the final we had worked on our shape in training and I was right-back with Marvin Elliott in midfield. As Dennis Wise was in Italy, coach Ray Wilkins took training. I was told I was in the team.

While no player would wish an injury on a team-mate, if it happens and you can benefit from this it is natural to think about yourself before others. I was hoping Wise would not be fit to play in Cardiff.

As much as anything, I had no fitness problems, having fully recovered from a knee injury I initially thought would prevent me from playing in the highest-profile game in domestic football.

When I was told Wise was '90 per cent certain' to miss the game I was consumed by a combination of excitement and nerves. While we were sworn to secrecy about team matters, I shared the news with my dad and we talked about how I was potentially going to stop Cristiano Ronaldo or Ryan Giggs.

My joy lasted just 48 hours because when Wise returned on the Thursday I was informed that he was going to start the game, play 20 minutes and then I would replace him. Elliott would begin at right-back and move into midfield when Wise came off.

This was not the end of the world as far as I was concerned. I'd still be playing 70 minutes of the final. Not many players achieve that.

Soon after the kick-off Wilkins told me to warm up as I'd probably be going on after 20 minutes.

I must have run up and down that sideline for 70 minutes waiting for my name to be called, but it never came.

Wise lasted 89 minutes despite being far from 100 per cent fit, but his experience enabled him to play through the pain barrier. Unless his leg was hanging off, he would play.

When he trudged off, Curtis Weston, not Alan Dunne, replaced him.

* * * * *

I PLAYED eight league games that season, and my only experience of cup football in 2003/04 was the 1-0 Carling Cup defeat by Oxford as an 88th-minute substitute. As it turned out, that was two minutes more than I was to play in our FA Cup run.

Kevin Muscat was the first-choice right-back and played in the earlier rounds of the FA Cup, but the Millwall captain was injured in the semi-final after a challenge with Sunderland's George McCartney left him requiring knee surgery. Dennis Wise hadn't seen the best of me and I had the impression he viewed me as more of a midfield player than a full-back.

For a club like Millwall, the main ambition in the FA Cup was to get a couple of relatively easy ties in rounds three and four and then draw a money-spinning game away to Manchester United, Chelsea or Arsenal in the fifth round. Or West Ham.

Reaching the final, especially against United, was the wildest of unrealistic dreams.

We started our unlikely road to Cardiff by beating Walsall, who finished with nine men, 2-1 at The Den in the third round thanks to goals from Tim Cahill and super Kevin Braniff.

In the fourth round the draw favoured us with a tie against Telford, a mid-table Conference side, albeit at their Bucks Head ground.

It was a big occasion for Telford to play a side from Division One – we would have been a prize scalp and they were a potential banana skin for us. It was like Telford's final in their small, tight ground and the fact it was the FA Cup lifted the atmosphere.

These games are rarely as easy as people think they should be. Smaller teams are desperate to make the headlines not just by knocking out a higher league side, but also because of the potential financial gains. A double which made the occasion a lot harder for Millwall.

Paul Ifill gave us the lead shortly before half-time and I remember sitting there thinking that having scored the first goal we should be okay.

Telford chased everything, but Wise knew what it took to win games like this through his experiences with Wimbledon and Chelsea, including winning the FA Cup in each of the previous three decades. He scored our second goal in the 83rd minute to give us a 2-0 win. Our biggest possible banana skin was averted.

Next up were Burnley at The Den and Danny Dichio, a new £500,000 signing from West Bromwich Albion, headed the only goal of the game from Muscat's cross. Dichio was not the most mobile of strikers but he was a good target man because he won so much in the air to set up chances for others with knock-downs.

Millwall had reached the FA Cup quarter-finals for the first time in 19 years and the feeling was, 'Let's get our big draw now. Manchester United or Arsenal away, please.'

When the balls were drawn out it was Millwall versus Tranmere.

The disappointment of missing out on playing either of English football's heavyweights lasted about five seconds because we were suddenly aware we had to beat a Division Two team for a place in the semi-finals. Ninety minutes from the last four with only Tranmere in our way, though as it turned out it was 180 minutes.

We had a chance to win at The Den but Muscat's penalty was saved by John Achterberg, so it was off to Prenton Park for the replay. A Dichio flick-on set up the main man Tim Cahill to open the scoring. Whenever we needed someone to produce something special Cahill was usually in the right place at the right time. He was blessed with a heading ability that belied his 5ft 10in frame. Cahill had incredible hang-time, almost defying gravity when the ball came to him.

It was Dichio, again, who paved the way for Neil Harris to make it 2-0 and though Gary Jones pulled one back for the lower league side, Wise's tactics were spot on and 27 games into his first managerial job he had led Millwall to their first semi-final in 67 years.

✳   ✳   ✳   ✳   ✳

I MAY have been a spectator, an unused sub, but the experience of being there, of watching, listening and learning, was immense, while the FA Cup run had put Millwall back on the map in the most positive of ways.

The other three semi-finalists were Manchester United and Arsenal from the Premier League and Sunderland, who, like us, were in Division One.

Millwall wanted Sunderland and Sunderland wanted Millwall – both our prayers were answered.

The fact that Sunderland's manager was Mick McCarthy who had previously been in charge of Millwall added extra spice to the game, not that it needed any.

We were at the training ground when the draw was made and like Sunderland, no doubt, we began thinking something that would have been ridiculous in January, 'We can reach the FA Cup Final.'

The match every young fan watches with his dad.

While United played Arsenal at Villa Park, Millwall headed for Old Trafford, a ground none of our players had ever visited, let alone played at. Theo Paphitis, our chairman, thought all his Christmases had come at once, loving and relishing the media attention.

There was never a chance of him saying his famous line from *Dragons' Den*, 'I'm out.'

Our league form suffered and any hopes we had of promotion vanished in the wake of our cup run because the semi-final became all-absorbing with camera crews from everywhere wanting a slice of Millwall. There was a terrific buzz around the training ground and Wise ensured morale was sky-high.

We went to Manchester on the Saturday, the day before the semi-final, and were given a tour of the stadium. We were like kids, taken in by the magic of the stunning home of United.

Going round the United dressing room and seeing where their superstars changed was a serious wow-factor. We may have been professional players about to take part in the FA Cup semi-final, but at heart we were simply football fans taken in by a scenario clubs outside the Premier League rarely experience. There was a presence, an energy in the United changing room. You could almost feel the winning mentality instilled by Sir Alex Ferguson.

I was not even on the subs' bench for the game, but I still warmed up with the team because Wise wanted the boys who did not make the 16 to be part of the whole experience. As the teams came out for the kick-off I walked down the tunnel behind them, almost feeling like I was a Manchester United player.

For a few seconds I was George Best.

As I reached the side of the pitch, the crowd, the noise, the atmosphere, the occasion and the sheer magnificence of the Theatre of Dreams are treasured memories.

Until the 26th minute it was a nothing game with both sides cancelling each other out. Then Cahill did what Cahill did so often and scored what proved to be the winning goal, not a trademark header, but a side-foot shot after Paul Ifill's effort had been parried by Mart Poom.

The bench erupted as Cahill took off his shirt and waved it in the air. But that was nothing like the celebrations when Paul Durkin blew the final whistle. We all joined in a lap of honour – well, nearly all of us because Cahill and Wise were surrounded by television cameras eager for their on-the-spot interviews.

I was proud to be part of a Millwall squad that had done what nobody believed possible.

In fact, something that no one had even thought about. It was my biggest achievement and, as players who were on modest salaries compared with our next opponents, the £15,000 bonus for reaching the final was very useful.

We also knew that we'd be in the UEFA Cup whatever the result in the Millennium Stadium as United, who had beaten Arsenal 1-0 in their semi, had qualified for the Champions League. Everyone was bursting with happiness and the journey home from Manchester in what became a party-coach was unforgettable.

Beers were taken on board though super Kevin Braniff and Dave Tuttle, who had not been involved in the game and had watched from the stand, had started their celebrations earlier and had hit the ground running. We were singing and dancing, a throwback to the way teams used to enjoy a huge win.

For reaching the FA Cup Final, Paphitis had promised he would take the players and their families to EuroDisney in Paris, all paid for by him. A truly marvellous gesture by the chairman. The spirit in the camp was raised, with everyone loving the moment.

To this day we are still waiting to go. He also promised us a watch each. We are still waiting for that, too.

I was pleased for Wise and his assistant, Ray Wilkins, a true gentleman. They both understood me, they knew what I was about and like Wise, I was a bit of a ticking time bomb. Wilkins was someone I had looked up to as a kid and now he and Wise were taking an interest in me, helping me with my career.

They made me feel like I was somebody.

✳   ✳   ✳   ✳   ✳

THE 2004 FA CUP FINAL was between the club tenth in Division One and the club who had finished third in the Premier League. One who had won the competition a record number of times against one who had been to only three semi-finals, in 1900, 1903 and 1937.

I had played in three league games towards the end of the season, but was injured against Coventry the week after the semi-final. I went in for a stupid tackle and came off second best, damaging medial ligaments in a knee. As I was carried off on a stretcher my immediate thought was that any chance of playing in the final, which was three weeks away, had gone.

I was gutted, but it was my own fault. I had gone in over-aggressively, it was a silly thing to do and I got what I deserved. I could not give myself the sympathy vote even though I believed my dream of being involved in the biggest match of my life was disappearing. Luckily I was wrong.

I returned in just over two weeks and with Kevin Muscat unavailable I was set to make my FA Cup debut for that season in the final against Manchester United. Football gets no better than that, well not when you're Alan Dunne.

The build-up was incredible. We were measured for our cup final suits made by designer Jeff Banks. The lining even had 'Millwall' printed on it. We had the lot – shirt, boxer shorts, socks, a belt, a hankie. I gave my suit to my dad though I'm not sure if he ever wore it. Or if it fitted him.

Then there was the FA Cup Final song called 'Oh Millwall' to the tune of Dean Martin's 'Volare' recorded at The Den.

It was cringeworthy. Imagine us singing:

'Oh Wisey…wo oh,
'La la la la la,

'Oh Wisey….wo oh oh oh,
'La la la la la la,
'He's only five foot four,
'And he'll make those Lions roar.'

Well, probably best that you don't imagine it, but for the record (excuse the pun) it broke into the UK top 75 at number 41, where it stayed for one week before disappearing without trace. But to be part of such a tremendous team spirit was a time you wanted to go on forever.

I NEVER thought we could win the FA Cup. Hoped, yes, dreamt, yes, but realistically we could not win. Manchester United had Cristiano Ronaldo, Ruud van Nistelrooy, Gary Neville, Roy Keane, Ryan Giggs and Paul Scholes. If we could keep them out for half an hour or so then who knows what might happen? But there was no logical argument I could put forward for a Millwall victory.

We had been extremely lucky with our run to the final, becoming the first team to reach it without playing a top-flight club. But this was Millwall's day out, a once in a lifetime experience for the players, our families and the fans.

The fact the game was at the Millennium Stadium and not Wembley was a little disappointing, but it was still an amazing ground.

TRAINING was intense during the week building up to the final with everyone wanting to impress and make the squad. In fact, things were so competitive that Mark McCammon and I almost came to blows. McCammon used to annoy me and I'd think, 'If you weren't 6ft 5in I'd knock you out.'

I was winding him up because I didn't think he was even a half-decent footballer. We were playing a five-a-side match and he kept giving the ball away. I was asking him, 'What the fuck are you doing?'

After training, McCammon pushed me and in retaliation I booted him. I also pushed him back. Big mistake. I then grabbed him by his throat. Bigger mistake.

It took six or seven of the lads to hold McCammon back. He said, 'I'll fucking kill you.'

I replied, 'Yeh, come on then,' praying that he would not break loose because he may well have killed me.

We sorted things out quickly enough and it was forgotten, though I remain grateful to this day the other lads restrained him.

McCammon had arms bigger than most people's legs, a chest as wide as the Grand Canyon and gave the impression that lifting a team coach would be a simple task.

✳ ✳ ✳ ✳ ✳

WE TRAVELLED down to Cardiff on the Thursday and I shared with midfielder Peter Sweeney, one of my closest mates at the time.

We used to room together and terrorise the older pros by changing numbers on their phones, hiding stuff, tying their shoelaces, and prank-calling their rooms. We were always up to something, but the victims liked us more because of this. It's all part of the world of football.

Our FA Cup Final suits were hung up in the wardrobe. It made us feel like Premier League stars.

However smart we looked on our way to the stadium, the match was as one-sided as just about everyone had predicted. Cristiano Ronaldo opened the scoring just before half-time after a mix-up between Dennis Wise and Neil Harris. A second-half brace from Ruud van Nistelrooy, one a penalty, completed United's comfortable victory.

I didn't indulge in any shirt-swapping even though many would regard a Manchester United FA Cup Final jersey as a special memory from the match. As my team had lost, I did not think I had a right to say, 'Can I have your shirt, please?'

While I respected the United players, it just wasn't in me to ask for a jersey. Maybe if I had played it would have been different, but under the circumstances – I was gutted I did not get on and that we had lost – I had too much pride for any shirt-swapping. Opponents' jerseys seem more to do with bragging rights than anything else and it is not something that interests me.

We were given two shirts by Millwall, one of which I kept while the other was auctioned for my testimonial. I am proud of my runners-up medal which is on display in my dining room because even though Millwall lost, I still felt I was part of something special for the only club I had played for.

I just wish I'd had a slightly bigger role in the game.

22

Skinhead stewards and wild supporters

Welcome to European football

MILLWALL'S first taste of European football included the most frightening, intimidating atmosphere I have experienced. Playing Ferencváros in the UEFA Cup first round in Budapest was unforgettable, if not necessarily for all the right reasons.

Reaching the FA Cup Final had guaranteed Millwall a place in the UEFA Cup as Manchester United had qualified for the Champions League.

Our opponents were Ferencváros, probably the most famous name in Hungarian football.

People talk about a game of two halves but Ferencváros were a club of two teams; the ordinary, fairly toothless opposition at The Den and the feisty, committed and highly motivated side at their own ground in the return.

There was a different atmosphere at The Den with a real European feel about it, unlike a domestic game. The bonus for getting past the Hungarians was far bigger than we would receive for a league win while for the club the financial potential was huge if we reached the group stage.

Dennis Wise gave us the lead with a superb curling free kick which he whipped round the end of the Ferencváros wall. They equalised, also from a set piece, but from what we had seen at The Den we flew to Budapest in an optimistic mood.

Little did we know what awaited us.

Driving to the stadium, every street seemed to be a natural home for graffiti artists. No wall was left unpainted. The police presence was enormous, so was the number of stewards who were more intimidating than any Ferencváros ultra. Each steward looked the same, like bodybuilders wearing a black puffa jacket, a shaved head and tattoos. They were mean-looking fuckers waiting for any Millwall fan to step out of line so they could rip his head off. They appeared more like trouble-makers than those whose job it was to keep the peace.

The stadium had high fences surrounding the pitch and it soon became obvious why such protection was necessary. The Ferencváros supporters were fanatical, really wild with flares going off and drums beating all the time while the crowd made it clear Millwall were not so much the opposition as the enemy. It was scary.

The home team were inspired by this partisan backing and each time Ferencváros attacked they looked like scoring. The transformation from the team we saw at The Den to the side we played on their own patch was remarkable.

Our players could not cope with an atmosphere unlike anything we had experienced previously.

I was a sub and we had been instructed to warm up behind a goal rather than running along the sideline as this was deemed too dangerous. The Ferencváros fans had been throwing small objects at us through the wire and it was just as well the fencing was strong as the supporters did their best to get at us.

I remember looking at the sea of fans standing up, chanting, singing and shouting. In the middle was one supporter wearing a white Republic of Ireland shirt. I have no idea whether he was Hungarian or Irish, but his jersey certainly stood out in a sea of Ferencváros supporters.

Maybe he was a fellow Dubliner who had found himself in the wrong end.

We still had to run the gauntlet of these supporters to reach our so-called safe area behind a goal to warm up. My worry was being hit by a dart. If, like me, you had watched a movie about hooliganism called *I.D.*, you will know darts were one of the weapons used. All I could think of was someone throwing a dart at me and being hit on the head.

I ran along the sideline with an arm covering my face, just in case.

Ferencváros didn't take any prisoners, either, totting up five yellow cards in each leg compared to Millwall's total of two.

We lost 3-1, going out 4-2 on aggregate. The excitement of a possible European bonus had disappeared.

I thoroughly enjoyed most of the experience, for all the dangers it posed and that we were outplayed in the second leg. It was wonderful to be part of playing in Europe, albeit briefly, travelling to a famous European capital, the hotel, the food.

Everything except the racism.

Sadly, this is not uncommon in Eastern Europe and Millwall complained to UEFA that Mark McCammon had been racially abused by Ferencváros fans as he warmed up.

The Hungarian club were fined £23,000 by UEFA, but escaped further punishment.

The British Embassy in Budapest also reported that two Millwall supporters were stabbed in disturbances before the match, but thankfully they were not seriously hurt. Chairman Theo Paphitis, who visited the two men in hospital, made his feelings known to UEFA.

He said, 'I have serious concerns about a number of issues surrounding this tie, including the provocation our supporters were subjected to inside the ground. Missiles were being thrown at us, our players were subjected to racial abuse and there was a lack of security where it was needed.'

Apparently, matches between Ferencváros and rivals Újpest are regularly marred by trouble. But I doubt if feelings between these clubs run higher than any match involving Millwall and West Ham.

23

Drunken West Ham fans in my face

I blew my chance of a statue at The Den

25 AUGUST 2009, WEST HAM v MILLWALL
The game both sets of fans wished for when the balls were drawn out for the second round of the Carling Cup. A match most players in their career may never experience. But if you have been fortunate enough to have played in such a derby, you will understand the hatred the two sets of supporters have for each other. The rivalry may sound ugly, but to play in such a nerve-tingling, knife-edge atmosphere is an experience like no other. The clash represents, at the same time, one of the biggest and least pleasant rivalries in football. Whether it is at The Den or Upton Park is almost irrelevant, Millwall want to play West Ham.

The rivalry, like all such match-ups, has escalated over the years and the Carling Cup tie underlined how hostile the feelings between the two sets of fans have become.

It will always be a game that attracts a huge police presence. Matches against Charlton, Crystal Palace, Luton Town, Cardiff City and Leeds United attract special atmospheres.

But West Ham are the real deal for Millwall. These games are like no other and are not for the faint-hearted.

* * * * *

A LASTING memory of the 2009 Carling Cup tie is the smell of alcohol as West Ham supporters invaded the pitch after an 87th-minute Junior Stanislas equaliser took the game to extra time. Neil Harris had scored with a superb volley in the 27th minute and we had held on for almost an hour before all hell broke loose.

Goodness knows how many West Ham fans ran on to the field to celebrate Stanislas's goal – the first of three such invasions. I was barged and pushed with grown men in my face, by one fan in particular whose weight was north of 20 stone. I remember him clearly because he was the spit of Minty from *EastEnders*.

The stench of booze all around me was so powerful it was like being in a pub. With the game being a 7.45pm kick-off the fans would, no doubt, have had plenty of time for their fair share of 'preparation'.

It was frightening to be surrounded by West Ham fans who hated Millwall and hated me because I played for the club. It made me think that all it needed in such circumstances is one nutcase on the field, drunk out of his skin, with no real control over his actions and hell bent on being a West Ham hero by attacking a Millwall player.

Would breaking the law, or even risking a potential jail term, stop such an attack? Maybe not and this crossed my mind amid the mayhem.

West Ham fans ran amok and I was just hoping no one would throw a punch as my immediate instinct may have been to react.

I would have felt obliged to defend myself in the same manner as if I had been attacked anywhere else outside football.

What is a player supposed to do in these circumstances? Let a drunken pitch invader just thump him? The law in football says yes. Striking a pitch invader could be deemed as a sending-off offence. A pissed-up fan hits a player, the player retaliates, red card.

I was unaware of any Millwall supporter running on to the pitch that night. However, the Football Association hit Millwall with three fan-related charges.

* * * * *

I DID NOT know Alan Baker before this League Cup tie, but he has since become a close friend. Al, as he is called, went to Upton Park with his two boys on the night of 25 August and was within an inch of losing his life after he was stabbed, the blade puncturing a lung.

Al went to watch a game of football and almost died.

Neil Harris knew little about the victim other than he was a Millwall fan. Being the sort of guy he is, Harris went to visit Al in hospital and was staggered to discover the supporter was someone he had met on holiday in Portugal a few weeks previously. We remain good pals and Al and his lovely family are regulars in the bar after games at The Den.

To the best of my knowledge, no one was ever charged for the attack on Alan Baker.

✳   ✳   ✳   ✳   ✳

I PLAYED at Upton Park three times during my Millwall career. The first was in September 2003, when we drew 1-1, Tim Cahill cancelling out David Connolly's opener. David James, Jermain Defoe and that fine, skilful defender Tomáš Řepka played that day. I was a young lad at the time and I was surprised when Mark McGhee selected me for such a big game in front of almost 30,000 spectators.

The atmosphere was hostile but the match ended without incident, though the police presence and the number of police horses on show was something very intimidating for such an inexperienced player.

My last visit, after the Carling Cup tie, came in February 2012 and was televised by Sky Sports. Millwall lost 2-1, failing to take advantage of Kevin Nolan's ninth-minute red card for a two-footed challenge on Jack Smith. My immediate reaction when Smith was fouled – I ran to the referee screaming, 'That's a straight red' – caused a brawl between both sets of players.

Emotions ran high and Nolan was given his marching orders. I was desperate to beat them and thought that as they were down to ten men so early in the match we'd have a better chance of winning.

Carlton Cole gave West Ham the lead with Liam Trotter equalising, but Winston Reid scored the winner after David

Forde had been fouled by Julien Faubert, though referee Mike Jones did not agree.

Like my first visit to Upton Park, there were no crowd problems.

THE BUILD-UP to the Carling Cup tie started at The Den where we had our pre-match meal before taking the coach through the Blackwall Tunnel, along the streets of east London and then on to Upton Park.

I was not initially in the starting XI, but Tony Craig failed a fitness test that morning. Kenny Jackett told me Craig was struggling and that I would be playing. I was buzzing.

The butterflies in my stomach were soon evident and my immediate thought was that if we won I had the chance to be a Millwall hero.

As the coach made its way towards the stadium the number of police vehicles was a reminder that this was more than just another match.

The sea of claret and blue shirts and pubs spilling over with screaming home fans added to the overriding feeling that West Ham versus Millwall is serious business. Outside the stadium is a statue of Bobby Moore and it was surrounded by hundreds, maybe even thousands, of West Ham fans.

Sitting in the coach and peering down on these supporters, I could almost feel the animosity towards Millwall.

I absolutely loved it. It is why I play football. This is what it's all about.

Passionate home fans can bang on the coach, while you do not have to be an expert lip-reader to know what they are saying. The West Ham supporters were kissing the badge on their shirts, many giving us a hand gesture similar to that of shaking a dice.

The only reaction can be to laugh and smile as this is merely the norm for every away team crossing enemy lines, especially when Millwall are in town.

AS THE Millwall coach pulled into Upton Park the atmosphere was electric. The most eagerly awaited Millwall game for years was less than a couple of hours away. I could feel the goosebumps.

I was first made aware that there was trouble outside when one of the match officials mentioned it. The referee, Paul Taylor, who had been pre-warned by the police, made a point of telling both teams not to over-celebrate after a goal for fear of antagonising either section of fans. He said the atmosphere would be very hostile so we should do nothing to raise the temperature even more.

Taylor told us he would do his best to manage the game accordingly, but no one should do anything daft like run towards the opposing fans to celebrate.

* * * * *

WHEN WE stood in the tunnel before the tie the noise level was sensational. Both sets of supporters were doing their best to set the scene for what was to come. 'Bring it on.'

It is always important never to show fear or weakness when Millwall are playing any opposition, but especially West Ham who were a Premier League scalp. I tried to make my body language as aggressive and confident as I could. All that was in my head was that we were going in to battle and I was prepared to do whatever it took to win.

A tunnel hug or whatever with an old team-mate is not for me, not that too many cross the divide between Millwall and West Ham.

I was proud to wear the Millwall shirt, always have been and I showed this sentiment to whoever we were playing. It's not a time to make friends.

When I shake hands with an opponent I try to grip him as hard as I can. I hate a soft handshake, which is so un-Millwall.

My dad always made sure from when I was a boy that I shook his hand like a man because he believes you can tell a lot from someone's handshake.

In football I think, 'I'm going to be playing against you in a few minutes – let the mind games start now.'

I'll usually look my direct opponent in the eye as I try to make a lasting impression on his right hand. If you think I'm bad, when David Forde shakes your hand, your arm almost comes out of its socket.

I know, because he did it pre-match to his Millwall team-mates.

❋   ❋   ❋   ❋   ❋

WHILE I had played in front of bigger crowds than the 24,492 at Upton Park that night, even 60,000 Wembley fans did not equal the level of noise that there was at this tie.

As the match kicked off a couple of early tackles fired the crowd up even more. Millwall were dominating the game, our tactics were working a treat with little Ali Fuseini, playing just in front of the back four, bossing the midfield.

Neil Harris's goal in the 26th minute, a stunning volley, was certainly not against the run of play. As soon as the ball went in the net, Chopper ran to the Millwall fans to celebrate in his trademark way, with one arm in the air. He was immediately surrounded by jubilant team-mates, though seconds later the ref was there saying, 'Enough, let's get back for the kick-off.'

Our fans were loving it and as the match progressed there was a realisation we could all become legends, being part of the first Millwall team to win a worthwhile game at Upton Park (the 2-1 victory in the Simod Cup in November 1987 doesn't count).

It was West Ham 0 Millwall 1 and I had the chance to make it 0-2.

I played a one-two with Chris Hackett, had another similar exchange with Gary Alexander before running with the ball towards the West Ham penalty area. After beating a defender, it was me against goalkeeper Robert Green and at that moment it flashed through my mind that I was on the verge of Millwall greatness.

I could score the goal that put the Carling Cup tie out of West Ham's reach. Had I done so maybe I, too, could have had a statue in my honour – but the statue stayed on hold.

Instead of striking the ball with everything I had, I tried to side-foot it past Green. There was no real conviction behind the shot and though the ball beat Green, it went wide of the post. No goal, a goal kick instead. And no statue.

I can use all sorts of excuses like being so far up the pitch was nosebleed territory for me. Maybe emotion takes over from the reality of the situation. I am more used to defending goals than scoring them. Perhaps I thought about the end process, the joy of scoring, rather than what I had to do.

These types of misses can be pivotal moments in games and so it proved as, with three minutes remaining, Junior Stanislas took advantage of a lapse in defensive concentration to equalise.

The West Ham supporters had become very frustrated – lovely – as Millwall had played well and dominated the ball for long periods. We were three minutes from glory when we gave away a poor goal, leaving Stanislas free on the far post to tap the ball home.

Having led West Ham for 61 minutes and with the final whistle three minutes away, it was like we had conceded the decisive goal rather than an equaliser.

The goal lifted the home crowd, while we were deflated at being so near, yet so far from a win no Millwall follower would ever forget.

Cue the first pitch invasion by West Ham fans and the game delayed by five minutes or so.

The second came after Stanislas made it 2-1 with a penalty and the third was registered when Zavon Hines scored West Ham's final goal.

The spot-kick was awarded when Frampton was adjudged to have handled the ball, but he was on the ground as the ball was hit with ferocity straight at him from close distance. It was hardly deliberate.

Hines's goal put any Millwall comeback out of reach.

When the referee blew for full time I just wanted to leave the pitch quickly and, above all, safely. I loved the rivalry, the atmosphere, what such a game means to the Millwall supporters and being part of it. But things got out of hand that night and at the final whistle, mounted police formed a barrier to ensure that the two sets of fans could not get at each other.

The police kept us in the stadium for two hours – 30 minutes longer than we were usually there after a game – and we were given a security escort as the Millwall coach left Upton Park.

I didn't sleep that night, such was the adrenalin and emotion after what had happened on and off the pitch.

It is never easy to just nod off after a match because of the sugar intake, the pre-game carbohydrates and caffeine, but that night it was impossible because of everything that had happened on and off the pitch.

* * * * *

A MONTH LATER the Football Association alleged that both clubs did not ensure their supporters conducted themselves in an orderly fashion 'in and around the ground' plus charges of failing to ensure their fans refrained from: violent, threatening, obscene and provocative behaviour; racist behaviour; throwing missiles, harmful or dangerous objects on to the pitch.

As I previously mentioned, I hadn't seen any Millwall fans run on the pitch at Upton Park.

The club were livid. Millwall officials had played no part in the pre-match security talks and had expressed their concerns about the ticketing arrangements.

While West Ham were fined £115,000, Millwall were cleared of all three charges. A belated but significant victory.

I was told that when a club is charged by the FA they still have to pay their own legal fees even if they are found not guilty.

Apparently, it cost Millwall £100,000 to mount their successful defence. Credit to chairman John Berylson, who paid for this out of his own pocket.

24

Day trippers spoil
FA Cup semi-final

Jackett is pushed over the edge

LOSING to Wigan Athletic in the FA Cup semi-final in 2013 was probably the day when Kenny Jackett realised his time as manager of Millwall was up.

There was crowd trouble during our 2-0 defeat – I remain unconvinced those responsible were diehard Lions, but because it was Millwall it was the only topic the media wanted to talk about. Jackett was proud that he had led a side who had struggled in the Championship to the last four of the FA Cup, but football came a poor second to the fighting at Wembley in the aftermath of the match.

Jackett is obsessed with football and when he was asked about the trouble after the game he replied, 'That's the first I've heard of it.'

He would have been so absorbed in the match he would not have been aware of anything going on in the stands.

That Millwall had reached the semi-finals was overlooked and the gaffer was hurt that the game and the team's achievements were barely mentioned. Nearly all the questions from the media were about off-field incidents.

Instead of talking about how well we had done to reach the last four, our tactics, what we did well and where we fell down, Jackett found himself discussing hooliganism.

I am sure that he would have been thinking about his future in the wake of our league form that season. Having served Millwall so well for five and half years, what happened at Wembley was the final nail in the coffin for him and I am sure made him decide he could take the club no further.

The headlines the following day were all about the crowd violence. Had it been any other club perhaps the coverage would not have concentrated on the trouble quite as much. Given Millwall's history the media's agenda was up and running. The press had a field day and once again Millwall were the subject of negative headlines.

Despite the defeat, it was a great achievement for us to reach the semi-finals, but all this was forgotten because of some people who were more likely to be day-trippers than true Millwall supporters. Jackett resigned a few weeks later, his departure no great surprise and probably cemented by what happened at Wembley.

NINE YEARS after reaching the 2004 FA Cup Final, Millwall began their 2012/13 campaign in the competition with a 1-0

win over Preston at The Den, Liam Feeney's first-half strike proving decisive. I didn't play – Adam Smith, who laid on the goal, was our right-back. I also missed the 2-1 victory over Aston Villa at The Den in the fourth round.

Villa had just been beaten in the Capital One Cup semi-final by Bradford City and I had a hunch they would not fancy coming to our place to play in front of our fans. Jackett had been keen for us to have a decent FA Cup run to make up for our generally disappointing league form and this was a good time to play a vulnerable Villa team.

Though Darren Bent gave Villa the lead with a scuffed shot, Danny Shittu equalised with a typical bullet header from James Henry's corner. With a minute remaining, John Marquis nodded Smith's cross past Shay Given. It was his first goal in 18 months so no wonder he didn't know how to celebrate. His team-mates did, though.

And so to the fifth round. Could Millwall get Manchester United? Arsenal? No, the FA Cup gods were against us because we were drawn to play Luton Town, again.

Inevitably, this regurgitated all the trouble from the 1985 FA Cup tie at Kenilworth Road, one of the darkest days in the history of Millwall and the famous old competition. As I was only two at the time I cannot talk about it with any first-hand knowledge.

I had played at the tight, compact Kenilworth Road a few times for the reserves so I had an idea of what to expect, though the build-up to the tie and what had happened 28 years earlier unsurprisingly gave the game more of a cutting edge than usual.

It made for a classic FA Cup tie with Luton of the Conference desperate for another big scalp after beating Wolves of the

Championship and the Premier League's Norwich in the two previous rounds.

I remember my mate Mick telling me he lost a watch during the fighting in 1985 and he said, 'If you could find it, that would be great.'

We knew the atmosphere would be hostile, while there were even reports that the game might be played behind closed doors as a security measure.

There was a massive police presence – even the coppers had subs, I think. I had won my place back from Smith and despite the crowd being just below 10,000 the noise was incredible. Luton had a few early chances, but once James Henry gave us the lead in the 12th minute we settled down and Rob Hulse made it 2-0 nine minutes before half-time.

Jackett was very good at knowing how to beat teams like Luton and Dany N'Guessan wrapped it up in the 86th minute. There was a good-natured pitch invasion at the final whistle with police dogs a big deterrent to anyone thinking of starting trouble. As I left the field with Henry, I playfully pushed him towards a police dog which television highlighted that evening.

The German Shepherd's reaction was what you would expect. Henry got some stick in the dressing room because he had a bit of a nose on him and we said that was the dog's target.

Oh, and I never found Mick's watch.

THE QUARTER-FINAL draw gave Millwall a third home tie against fellow Championship team Blackburn Rovers, who had beaten Arsenal at the Emirates. The game at The

Den was goalless, a fair result though I had a big bust-up with Andy Keogh after he went for glory late in the match and missed rather than passing to me when I was in a much better position to score. I was angry that he was selfish while believing if we were going to beat Blackburn it was going to be at The Den. I did not fancy a midweek replay at Ewood Park.

My frustration spilled over in the dressing room and things became very heated between us. I lost my head and told Keogh to fuck off out of the club and take his missus with him.

Something seemed to have happened to Keogh and the impression was that his private life was affecting his football which was suffering because of this. He was last in for training, the first to leave and was so quick to shower and change.

It takes most of us three-quarters of an hour after coming off to shower, dry ourselves, dress and what have you. Republic of Ireland international Keogh seemed to do all this in a couple of minutes.

Our insults became personal to the extent Keogh stood up, ready for a fight. I said, 'Sit down you fanny. What are you going to do?'

I texted him later to apologise for some of the things I had said. I felt bad and it became personal, but I don't think the apology went down too well.

Keogh wasn't a bad lad. It was just a build-up of frustration during the game and things were said in the heat of the moment which I later regretted.

Three days later, despite my misgivings, we beat Rovers 1-0 in the replay at Ewood Park, Danny Shittu's first-half header – was it in his contract he could only score with headers? – ensuring Millwall's place in the semi-finals.

Before the game, big Dan put the fear of God into Jordan Rhodes. Danny would always stand near the front and scream at the opposition, trying to intimidate them. 'COME ON... COME ON...IT'S WORK TIME...IT'S WORK TIME.'

Yelling like the beast he was, the big man said, 'Where are you Jordan Rhodes? I'm coming to get ya. I want ya. I'll take a yellow for ya.'

Rhodes was nowhere to be seen, the last player out of the dressing room as we walked on to the pitch. He had a very quiet game, one of many Blackburn players to freeze on the night while Millwall rose to the occasion.

Afterwards, Danny and I did a live interview with Sky Sports in the dressing room, the chat not made any easier by socks being thrown at us and other things going on best left to your imagination.

Danny ended the interview with his trademark catchphrase, 'That's what we do, that's what we do.'

✳ ✳ ✳ ✳ ✳

THE FOLLOWING Saturday, we beat Charlton 2-0 and what better way to end a super week for the club than celebrating St Patrick's Day on the Sunday?

Liam Feeney, whose parents are both Irish, and Republic of Ireland under-21 international Shane Lowry telephoned me about going to Waxy O'Connor's in the West End.

We took the train to London and joined the queue outside the pub. Two minutes later who should turn up?

Andy Keogh and his wife. For fuck's sake. Don't talk to me about the luck of the Irish. There were so many people in the line it was an hour before we got in. Having to stand there for 60 minutes and make small-talk with Keogh and his missus was uncomfortable, putting it mildly. I don't think Keogh had told his wife about our little altercation, but suffice to say the conversation did not exactly flow like the Guinness did later on.

I should not have said what I did, but in the heat of the moment such things happen.

KENNY JACKETT had the good FA Cup run he had hoped for. The next stop was Wembley and Wigan in the semi-finals – as Chelsea played Manchester City in the other semi Millwall probably had the best chance we could of reaching a second final in nine years.

It was the second time I had played at Wembley, my first being the 2009 League 1 Play-Off Final against Scunthorpe United when we lost 3-2. The game was watched by a crowd of 59,661, including about 50,000 Millwall followers.

It was the hottest day of the year and as we walked down the tunnel the thermometer was showing 104 degrees. As if this wasn't enough, there were two flame-shooters waiting for us pitchside.

One almost singed my eyebrows and the heat was so extreme it was like landing in the Sahara Desert.

The noise, the atmosphere, the sight of our fans put me in a sort of trance. I think the occasion got to us. The build-up, special club suits, the media attention, we lost focus of what we needed to do on the pitch to win the game. We were well below par on the day and at the final whistle, as much as I wanted to savour the occasion, I disappeared straight down the tunnel.

I didn't even want to go to the after-match party. The loss and our display hit me so hard I was distraught for a month following the game. Our whole season had come down to one match and we had blown it. I was gutted, even depressed, and kept asking myself, 'What if. What if?'

But you cannot change what has happened and credit to Jackett who led us back to Wembley the following year and this time Millwall beat Swindon 1-0 to win promotion to the Championship, though I was injured for that game.

✻　✻　✻　✻　✻

FOR OUR semi-final against Wigan, we had a couple of injuries which meant some players had to play out of position, square pegs in round holes. Ideally Millwall needed to be at full strength and playing to our peak against a well-drilled Wigan side managed by Roberto Martínez.

We knew Callum McManaman, Shaun Maloney and James McCarthy would have to be stopped, but we gave away a sloppy goal to Maloney in the 25th minute and again too many of our players froze on the day. While Wigan had their eyes on the prize, Millwall were just happy to be there, not really believing we'd make the final.

Wigan had that belief whereas we felt we'd done the hard work by reaching Wembley and played the occasion rather than the game, which we lost 2-0.

I was aware of something happening in the crowd because I heard booing and other noises, but I had to keep my focus. At one point I noticed police going into a stand though I had no idea of what was happening.

Reports said 14 spectators were arrested, 12 allegedly supporting Millwall and two from Wigan. Some of the addresses of the alleged Millwall fans arrested were distinctly un-Millwall heartlands. I believe they were a group of day-trippers who went too far. Some of the trouble-makers were just in front of my dad and my wife and it was not just alcohol that these idiots took on board.

They were not part of the Millwall faithful, not Den regulars or those who loved the club.

Millwall have done so much, all they could, to keep hooligans and thugs away from the club, but they were powerless to stop clowns like those at Wembley doing what they did on the day. They have worked closely with local communities though Millwall remain an easy target for 'sensational' media coverage.

One tabloid sent a reporter to The Den when Millwall played Brighton and he wrote that there were chants of 'Sieg Heil' by home fans. Close. It was 'Seagulls' by the Brighton supporters. The reporter was forced to make a grovelling apology.

Millwall have a zero tolerance towards racism and have banned more offenders than any other club.

Again, chants by the fans who love Jimmy Abdou – they sing 'AbDOU…AbDOU' – were misinterpreted as monkey chants, for Christ's sake.

25

Captain Dunne

*After calling some team-mates c***s*

THE STAFF meeting two days before the start of 2014/15 was over. Ian Holloway had gathered everybody who worked for the club together to project his vision for Millwall, how he saw the future, how he wanted us to be respected as a club and to change the public's view.

Afterwards, Ollie pulled me to one side and said, 'Alan, can I have a word?' We walked to a quiet room where he sat me down.

'Dunney,' he said. 'I want you to be my captain.' For once I was speechless.

The gaffer told me that I was the right man. I had not let him down since his arrival and had been nothing less than professional after he succeeded Steve Lomas. During the previous season, I didn't show disappointment or throw a strop when he brought in Ryan Fredericks from Spurs on loan – another right-back. Holloway told me how he'd been following the young boy for some time and that Fredericks fitted the style of play he wanted, with his full-backs operating like wingers when they went forward.

Not the best of starts for me with the new manager.

It was devastating to hear that the gaffer was bringing in someone to probably replace me, though it was something previous managers had said to me many times. I'd always been able to rise to the challenge and see off potential successors. Once again I did what I had always done which was to get my head down, keep quiet, support whoever it was who came in and try my hardest to win my place back.

Over the years there had been so many right-backs brought in to challenge me. To name a few, there was Kevin Muscat (Rangers), Adam Smith and Ryan Fredericks from Tottenham, Arsenal's Justin Hoyte, Richard Duffy (Portsmouth), Ryan Green (Wolves), Sergei Baltacha (St Mirren), the father of Elena, the former English tennis number one who died in May 2014, Danny Senda (Wycombe), Maurice Ross (Wolves), Marcus Bignot (QPR), Jack Smith (Swindon) and Matt Lawrence (Wycombe).

There was also a young Glen Johnson who spent three months at Millwall on loan from West Ham in 2002.

Johnson wasn't getting a game for West Ham who were struggling in the Premier League. My form for Millwall had dipped and Johnson came in on loan and played a few matches for us. He did okay, though there was little evidence that he would eventually become an established England international.

He returned to Upton Park having benefited by playing eight matches for Millwall. Johnson made his West Ham debut and played 15 games as they escaped relegation.

I would say Johnson has a lot to thank Millwall for. It's always nice to help your biggest rivals.

In these types of situations some players become disgruntled and may even try to disrupt team spirit, spreading negativity through the squad. Being a bad apple has never been my style and Ollie appreciated that one of his senior players acted professionally rather than being a frustrated trouble-maker.

To be made captain by someone as experienced, honest and real as Ian Holloway filled me with pride.

I texted my dad and my wife to tell them the news. Dad lives for my football and we'd shared tough times together when Millwall were struggling, speaking for hours. Dad always calls defeats or bad spells 'like stab wounds'.

You have to take the knife out and get on with it.

This time, he was overjoyed at the news and couldn't begin to tell me how proud he was.

My immediate thought was that I did not want to let the manager down. Captaincy brought an added pressure and I was determined to help the gaffer, the team and the club succeed. If that didn't happen it would reflect badly on me. Success or failure cannot be placed on the shoulders of one player, but in football you are judged by what you achieve. It is a results-led business and rightly or wrongly, the captain tends to get extra credit when the side wins and more blame in defeat.

I did not want to be known as a losing captain as the 2014/15 Championship season began.

✳   ✳   ✳   ✳   ✳

FOUR MONTHS EARLIER Millwall were staring relegation in the face. Birmingham City had beaten us 3-2 at The Den on 25 March and four days later ten-man Blackburn Rovers – I didn't play in this match – had scored in the last minute to snatch a 2-2 draw. Next up was a trip to Nottingham Forest who had hopes of a play-off place.

With seven games to play I could see no way out for Millwall. I was convinced we were heading for League 1. We were doomed. The relegation clock was ticking.

To prepare for the trip to the City Ground, Ian Holloway organised a nine-a-side first team versus the reserves game. I was in the reserves and we won 6-0.

While fringe players may give a little bit extra in such practice matches, when the score reached 6-0 the manager called the game off. Enough was enough. In the changing room he said, 'I cannot have my first team being beaten 6-0 by the reserves.'

I looked around the dressing room and thought, 'Do some here actually give a fuck? I will lose 25 per cent of my wages if Millwall are relegated.' That was in our contracts and is a lot of money for my family to do without.

More than anything, I did not want Millwall to go back into League 1.

There were players picking up big salaries and those on loan would return to their parent club unaffected. Team-mates had their heads down, no eye contact, staring at the floor in silence.

This was my future. My livelihood. My job. My club.

Millwall meant everything to me. I did not want to return to the third tier of English football and at that moment I could see no way out. Everything pointed to the drop; the results, the body language, the wrong attitude of some in the squad.

I had to say something and I did, using the c-word several times – and I don't mean chum.

I said, 'If we go down how many of you can honestly put your name on the board and say you'll be here next season? Half of you c***s will go back to your own clubs on your wages and others will look to fuck off because you won't want to play in League 1 if we go down.

'So tell us now, I'll put my name up first, but who doesn't want to stay here? Speak up and let the rest of us who do fight for Millwall.'

My emotions and feelings for the club were such that my eyes welled up. I was so hurt by Millwall's position. What I did was spontaneous, it was not to earn brownie points from the manager, I just cared so much, so deeply for Millwall and I spoke from the heart.

My intention was not to hurt anybody, I just wanted to get across how passionate I felt about where we were and how we had to find it within ourselves to battle like never before to keep the club in the Championship.

I don't think Holloway had ever heard anyone speak like this. When I had finished the room fell silent again. I walked out and headed towards the showers. I remember David Forde being the first to say to me, 'What you said was right.' Some others players said the same.

But words are cheap, we needed action and Holloway provided that.

✳ ✳ ✳ ✳ ✳

THE MANAGER made seven changes to the side that had drawn with Blackburn. When Nottingham Forest saw our team sheet they must have thought their luck was in. The gaffer took a huge gamble with his team selection and regardless of the result or what may have happened subsequently, he wanted honesty and absolute hard work. Total graft and then some.

It was almost as if Ian Holloway was saying, 'We might be relegated, but I am going to make my point for next season. I am only going to select players who show me they want to be here for the club.'

The wholesale changes made by the gaffer for the Forest game was a brave tactical move that worked. There was an improved attitude in the side, with experienced players like myself and Nicky Bailey setting a tone that hopefully rubbed off on the youngsters. After earlier misgivings about playing in the centre, I felt comfortable in the role. The team began to dominate the ball more and there was an energy change that eventually saw us to safety.

I was reinstated, moving from right-back to the centre of defence – I had never played centre-half in a first-team game before. Kenny Jackett had wanted to try me there, but at the time I did not have the confidence to make the switch. I was worried that I was not big enough to handle the physical side of playing against some man-mountain strikers. With more experience I felt comfortable moving inside.

After we had survived, Jackett texted me to say, 'I told you five years ago you could be a central defender.' I think he was trying to take the credit for it.

Ollie's view was that I had not believed in myself enough and he would change that mindset. 'I am going to make you a better player and then you'll see how good you can be,' he said. 'You can be one of the top central defenders in this league.'

The gaffer was correct. Football is not just about ability, it is also about belief.

* * * * *

AT THE City Ground I was handed the captain's armband in the absence of Paul Robinson, who was a substitute. Millwall beat Nottingham Forest 2-1 and there was a feeling of togetherness with our brilliant travelling fans that had been absent for too long.

Victory at Wigan was followed by a draw against Watford and three points at Middlesbrough. A frustrating goalless draw at The Den against Doncaster was a minor setback because we then came away from Queens Park Rangers with a valuable point.

Our last game of the season was at home to Bournemouth and we were not mathematically safe.

It was a similar scenario to 2013 when we lost 1-0 at Derby in the final fixture. I think for a five-minute spell we were going down as the scores of the other teams battling against relegation chopped and changed. Crystal Palace, managed by Holloway, did us a favour by beating Peterborough 3-2, Mile Jedinak scoring an 89th-minute winner, which helped us survive that year.

Thanks, Ollie.

This time our fate was in our own hands and coming off a six-game unbeaten run, we were on a roll with our confidence high. To blow it all in the last match, especially at home, would have been heart-breaking, but as soon as I led the team out of the tunnel – my kids, Lola and Shay, walked out with me – the noise level and the incredible support from our fabulous fans told me we would finish the job.

I believe we could have played anyone that day and beaten them, such was the atmosphere, the energy, the passion and the feeling inside The Den.

Bournemouth had enjoyed a good season under their excellent manager Eddie Howe and at one stage looked as if they could make the play-offs. I was nervous because the final day of fixtures has a habit of throwing up unexpected results, though there was an inner confidence throughout the side after the unbeaten run we'd been on.

It took us 27 minutes to break the deadlock through Martin Woolford and despite having only the slenderest of leads, we were comfortable and generally in control.

We beat Bournemouth 1-0 and survived by four points after winning 15 out of a possible 21 points in our last seven matches.

When referee Michael Naylor blew the final whistle there was a huge feeling of relief that we would be in the Championship again the following season. Had Steve Lomas remained in charge I think we would have been relegated. I sensed a month after Lomas arrived that we could struggle.

During the week Lomas was more the player than the manager – he had all the banter, joined in the training, he was maybe too much part of the team. He found it difficult to separate himself from his days as a player to being a manager. I feel when a manager becomes too involved with the players on a daily basis they pick up on weaknesses.

So on a matchday when Lomas had to distinguish himself as a manager it wouldn't work. The players would feel too comfortable and because of this I didn't think he got the best out of the group.

On the other hand I realised from Holloway's initial team meeting that Millwall had a manager who would inspire confidence.

❋ ❋ ❋ ❋ ❋

THERE was another reason Millwall survived the drop that season – a goldfish. Yes, a lucky goldfish.

A close friend of mine, Tommy Pratt from Southwark Metals, had a serious fear of flying so he went to see Nik and Eva Speakman who help people with anxiety issues and phobias.

They showed Tommy a film about a girl with an irrational fear of fish who had fallen into the sea.

The girl could not touch or even look at a fish because when she fell into the sea the first thing she saw was lots of fish. She panicked and this haunted her for many years. Nik and Eva explained to her that it was not the fault of the fish so why blame them? It may seem funny, but the logic really helped Tommy to understand his fear of flying.

When I texted him to ask how the meeting went, he replied, 'Don't blame the fish.'

My first thought was that Tommy had probably lost his marbles.

And then came, 'May the fish be with you.'

He's definitely lost them.

❋ ❋ ❋ ❋ ❋

AIMEE WAS organising a party for Tommy's mother's 70th birthday at the Dorchester Hotel. The day before, Tommy was asked by the manager if there was anything else he wanted, anything at all. 'We'll get it in for you, sir,' said the manager.

Of all the things the staff at the Dorchester have been asked for by the rich and famous, I doubt whether they have ever had a request for a goldfish.

I kid you not and at the dinner the next night, on Tommy's table, there was a big old goldfish. The name given to the fish was: Fish.

Having survived being fed bread – albeit Dorchester bread – and spending the night in a penthouse suite, the fish – or Fish – was about to become Millwall's lucky mascot.

Without fail, before each of the remaining games Tommy would text me and David Forde to say, 'May the fish be with you.'

It was the beginning of April and Millwall went on an unbeaten run. Seven texts, seven games without defeat. A coincidence? Who knows?

On one occasion the goldfish looked like his life had come to a premature end, but Tommy took it out of its bowl, blew in its face, returned it to the water and hey presto, it was soon swimming around again.

In the last game we had to beat Bournemouth to avoid relegation. Such was the importance of the match Tommy brought the fish to his box at The Den.

Like the fish, Millwall survived and finished in 19th plaice.

* * * * *

I HAD RETAINED the captaincy for the last seven games, but when we returned for pre-season before the start of 2014/15 Ian Holloway was very coy about the identity of the new permanent skipper in succession to Paul Robinson, who had joined Portsmouth on loan.

In press conferences the manager talked up Nicky Bailey and David Forde as possible captains, playing my chances down, perhaps to see how I would react. I think he wanted me to show it was not a seven-game fluke and that I was worthy of the honour full-time.

I felt I deserved to be captain. Had the gaffer chosen Bailey or Fordey I would have respected the decision, though not necessarily agreed with it.

❉   ❉   ❉   ❉   ❉

BEING THE captain of a club gives you extra respect throughout football and that is something I was very proud of. Having spent most of my life at Millwall as a fan and a player, to be made captain was the highlight of my career.

The responsibility was something I had dreamed of and whatever the pressures, it was still a challenge I would much rather have had than not.

As the team's leader I tried not to become detached from the other players or act as though I was above them. I still joined in the dressing-room banter, but there remained a heightened awareness that I was representing the club as captain. There had to be a line in the sand.

The younger players tend to look up to you and as captain I took a more hands-on approach to try to help them. When Matthew Briggs was sent off on his debut against Wycombe

I was going to lose my head after the game and tell him how unprofessional he had been to remove his shirt after scoring what turned out to be the winner in the 27th minute. Whether we agree with this law or not, we all know it is a mandatory caution.

Briggs was then shown a second yellow card in the 59th minute for a reckless challenge so we had to play the last third of the game with ten men. He apologised before I could blow a gasket so I felt it was not fair to erupt at him though I am sure the matter would have been dealt with by the manager.

If you score the winner in the last minute of the World Cup Final and remove your jersey to celebrate, fine. But to do it 27 minutes into a Carling Cup second round tie against Wycombe, no.

It was one of the silliest things I had seen in football, but a lot of emotions came out due to Briggs's previous experience at Fulham who loaned him out four times in three years.

AS CAPTAIN, I was allowed to ask the referee questions relating to a decision, though if three or more players (since reduced to two) from a side confront the match official and he feels harassed, the club run the risk of being fined. This happened to Millwall during one match in 2013/14 and the club were hit with a Football Association fine of £16,000.

If a referee is surrounded by dissenting players it looks ugly. It may be a natural reaction if you think the ref has made a mistake, but he never changes his mind because players tell him he was wrong. Mind you, some teams are better at pressurising the referee than others. They know how many should go to the ref and they rotate the players who query his decisions to minimise the risk of a yellow card for dissent.

Another responsibility I had as captain was to be in charge of the club fines. I had to keep a note of players who had been hit in the pocket for being late or for on-field indiscretions and how much it had cost them.

The money went into a pot and at Christmas a charity benefited with some going towards staff bonuses.

✳   ✳   ✳   ✳   ✳

I WAS OFTEN asked what I said during our pre-match huddle. It varied from game to game. Most of all, in the 15 or 20 seconds available you have to make sure you do not say the same every week. I tried to highlight something that could happen early in the match, maybe 'don't get blocked on set pieces against this lot', or 'let's steam into them from the off'. In a short space of time I wanted to get the team up for the battle ahead while making a relevant tactical point.

Set pieces are massive these days and having to defend one in the first minute can catch a team cold.

Goalmouths can see holding, pushing, shirt-tugging, it's called the Italian way of marking, which is tight going on cuddling.

Players with top Premier League clubs are past masters at such dubious arts and are able to get away with it a lot more. The more experienced you are, the easier it becomes to defend, one way or another, corners and free kicks.

Teams know who the dangermen are in such situations and what they are capable of. Like any other defender, there have been occasions when I have pulled an opponent down, but with so much going on the match officials haven't seen it. While the ball is not in play you cannot concede a penalty which is why the pulling and pushing can stop once the corner is taken.

Rickie Lambert is brilliant at set pieces. He will allow you to mark him tightly and when the ball is played in he will push you to gain a yard on you. It may sound easy and straightforward, but it isn't and I have not come across anyone who does it better.

Some teams mark zonally at set pieces so players are only responsible for a certain area. If the ball goes elsewhere a player stays where he is because it's not in his zone. I prefer marking players so everyone has a responsibility.

You know which opponent is your man so there should be no misunderstandings.

IN CERTAIN respects taking over as Millwall captain from Paul Robinson was difficult. It was a double-edged sword. The captaincy made me immensely proud, but at the same time Robbo had been a friend since I was 15 and we remain close today. I'd played with him throughout my Millwall career and I knew what the armband meant to him.

He shook my hand and said 'well done' but it was a little uncomfortable to see a Millwall legend like Robbo lose the captaincy. However, the game moves on and it was my turn.

Alan Dunne, captain of Millwall. Dreams do come true sometimes though not always with a happy ending.

26

I would have loved to have been a boy in green

My record in the Championship should have earned me an Ireland cap

ONE OF THE goals I never achieved is playing for the Republic of Ireland. I would have loved to have won just one cap for my country, even as a last-minute substitute on a cold night away to Kazakhstan.

The nearest I have been was a chat with a Scot who spoke to a Welshman.

When Mark McGhee was Millwall manager, his assistant Archie Knox, a Scot who was well connected in the game, liked my style, my fighting spirit. One day as he drove me back to The Den after training – I think it was in 2002/03 – our chat turned to international football.

He asked me if I had ever played for Ireland at any level. I told him that I had not and he said he would have a word with Ian Evans, the former Wales international who was Mick McCarthy's assistant, and put a word in for me. Knox believed I was worth a chance.

I remember Ally McCoist saying on television that two young players to watch out for were Theo Walcott, then of Southampton, and Alan Dunne. Toby Porter of the *South London Press* did a story about this and I had a lot of other media attention. My form was good and inevitably what Knox and McCoist said raised my hopes and expectations.

My head was spinning and Johnny Mac, my agent, started talking big dough that I could earn. I thought I had made it before I had even been there.

Neil Warnock spoke about possibly signing me after I had enjoyed two outstanding games against Sheffield United. On both occasions I had skinned David Unsworth, the Blades' left-back, to the extent he was substituted.

I took my foot off the gas and a month later I was injured, with Ireland becoming a dream that sadly remains that.

Ireland manager Giovanni Trapattoni never watched Millwall, or, indeed, attended many matches in England when he was in charge. It is a long time since Ireland could cherry pick from Manchester United, Arsenal and Liverpool and in recent years a number of their players have been with Championship clubs.

I never had word that Trapattoni or any of his representatives had watched Millwall, which is poor.

Martin O'Neill had a higher awareness of Irish players in the Championship while his assistant, Roy Keane, had first-hand experience of football at this level from his time as manager of Sunderland and Ipswich. Teams who are relegated from the Premier League often struggle in the Championship, whose clubs have caused many a cup upset against those in the top league.

I think there is little between the bottom eight of the Premier League and the top eight in the Championship. A popular belief is that the Championship is not particularly strong which is possibly because television-wise the Premier League dominates and people are almost brainwashed into believing anything else is second-rate.

It is unusual for a player who is eligible for Ireland to play as many games as I did in the Championship and not receive a call-up. Other defenders have had a brief taste of international football despite being outside the top flight.

Joe O'Cearuill won two caps in 2007 while on loan to Brighton. Eddie Nolan made his Ireland debut against Nigeria in 2009 when on loan to Preston North End from Blackburn Rovers. Jim Goodwin won his only cap as a substitute away to Finland in 2007 while playing for Scunthorpe.

Stephen O'Halloran made his Ireland debut in 2007 despite not having played a single first-team match for Aston Villa. Alan Bennett had not made his Reading debut following his move from Cork City when he won the first of two Ireland caps the same year. Alex Bruce was an Ipswich player when he made his Ireland debut, also in 2007, before switching his allegiance to Northern Ireland.

Maybe you need a little bit of luck, to be on top form in a big game when injuries force call-ups for new faces.

Although it looks like my time has passed, I still have the dream that one day, even for just one game, I'll become one of the boys in green.

I would have loved to have been a boy in green

❋   ❋   ❋   ❋   ❋

PERHAPS the nearest I shall get is Euro 2016 because, tickets and time permitting, I hope to be in France cheering on my country. My accent may betray my place of birth but I am 100 per cent Irish and though I like England to win, nothing can match the thrill of seeing Ireland victorious. Though to be in the Marriott Hotel, Waltham Cross, with my Leyton Orient team-mates on a bonding week was an unusual place to celebrate the play-off victory over Bosnia & Herzegovina in November 2015.

Like most Ireland supporters, I was pessimistic about our chances of qualifying after the home draw with Scotland. They say 'you'll never beat the Irish' – well, Scotland did in Glasgow, but Germany couldn't manage it in two ties and the victory over the world champions in Dublin changed everything.

Martin O'Neill and Roy Keane deserve every bit of praise that has come their way. Ireland do not have players to match the Germans, though the pair have instilled a spirit, belief, determination and pride in the team that means they do not go out and hope not to lose as they did under Trapattoni. They think they can beat anyone.

David Forde played most of the qualifying ties, including the draw in Germany, but lost his place towards the end of the campaign. Three Ireland goalkeepers, Fordey, Shay Given and Rob Elliot, are all reserves for their clubs but each has shown they can do a job when called upon.

I know Fordey is proud to have been part of Ireland's qualification for Euro 2016 and desperately wants to be part of the squad for the finals.

Hopefully, I'll be there to cheer on the boys in green.

27

The naked truth about toast

An expensive lesson in buying a stolen TV

MY RELATIONSHIP with the media has generally been good. The two local papers closest to Millwall, the *South London Press* and the *Southwark News*, give the club extensive coverage with fair criticism when needed. I was always happy to help the *SLP*'s Millwall correspondent and sports editor Toby Porter plus Jim Lucas and his successor on the *SN*, Alex Aldridge, who now works for the club.

Inevitably with so many right-backs brought in over the years my future was cast in doubt, but they had a job to do and I appreciated that. I have always made a point of being honest with the press rather than talk in clichés and certainly never lied because that can come back and bite you.

Millwall have tended to attract headlines for the wrong reasons and rarely receive the credit for things they do for the right reasons. There have been too many unproven accusations of racism with certain players using this to publicise themselves.

However, the area of football reporting that can cause most arguments is the marks given to players at the end of a match report. I cannot see how a reporter can watch maybe 28 players so thoroughly he can credibly say how many out of ten each deserves.

I remember David Forde receiving what he thought was a low mark in one particular newspaper.

He confronted the football writer responsible and for the next six Millwall matches the journalist in question reported on, he made Fordey the star man.

I was asked to appear on Sky Sports when Ian Holloway was appointed Millwall manager. We were filming outside the David Lloyd Leisure Centre in Beckenham and as it was raining I was given a Sky Sports umbrella which just happened to be red and blue. I received merciless abuse on social media from Crystal Palace fans claiming that I was a closet Palace supporter.

If that wasn't bad enough, when Sky Sports publicised the interview it said 'Alan Dunne' with a photograph of Jack Smith, who was with Millwall from 2009 until 2014. It wasn't the first or last time this had happened.

Some of my best media coverage has been with Jack Smith's photo. How easy it is to get two skinheads confused.

My debut as a Sky Sports studio pundit was for Millwall's home game against Cardiff in October 2014 when I was suspended. I'm not sure why, but I was very nervous and didn't really feel comfortable, probably because it was a small broadcasting area and quite claustrophobic plus I had a face full of make-up.

It also played on my mind that there was no delay in going out as there is on radio, so this was live in every sense of the word. People told me I looked at the floor too much – in fact, there were three TV monitors down there, one showing replays, so I watched them to help me.

However, it was a wonderful experience and has prompted me to do a media training course in the near future.

* * * * *

I KEPT a very low profile while I was on holiday in Dubai after being told Millwall were not offering me a new contract, apart from a wind-up with Toby Porter of the *South London Press*. I was in a restaurant with my good mate Tommy Pratt, former team-mate Gary Alexander and Millwall goalkeeper David Forde.

We'd had a few cocktails and it was then when Tommy suggested a bit of banter by telling Porter, who had been phoning me constantly, I was in Dubai to sign for a club in Qatar.

The plot was hatched. I phoned Porter and told him what was [not] going on – 'I'll call you again tomorrow and you can have the exclusive.'

Porter texted me back, saying he needed to speak now.

Alexander pretended to be Jason Mac, the son of Johnny who was once my agent. Pratt was Sheikh Mahumamady, the owner of Al Jazera. The part of Alan Dunne was played by Alan Dunne.

'Toby,' I said. 'I don't have long. I'm sitting here with my agent.'

'Who? Johnny Mac?'

'No, his son Jason who is looking after me now. I am signing tomorrow.'

In the background Tommy started to gabble away in so-called Arabic, trying his best to sound agitated. I said, 'Toby, he thinks you are someone trying to prise me away from Al Jazera.' Then me to Tommy, 'It's okay sheikh, he's a reporter I know who wants the exclusive.'

I then handed the phone to 'Jason Mac' and Alexander said, 'It's a three-year deal. He's on 30,000 dirhams a week [just over £5,000], plus a car and an apartment.'

Tommy then interrupted in his best Arabic with Mac, sorry I mean Alexander, saying, 'It's okay, he's a journalist in London.' After ten minutes we could not continue as we were laughing so much, but we had Porter hook, line and sinker. Ish.

Of course, I was never going to let Porter print this, but when I phoned him back he was ahead of the game. 'You almost had me,' he said. 'I thought I'd phone Johnny Mac because I could not find a team called Al Jazera.'

Needless to say, Mac had no idea what Porter was talking about.

'I spoke to your son, Jason.'

'Jason is with me now.'

Johnny put Jason on the phone and the stitch-up was confirmed. There is a club called Al Jazera in Abu Dhabi in the United Arab Emirates, but not in Qatar. Porter took it well and in return I gave him what he had really wanted – the exclusive about my departure from The Den.

* * * * *

THE ONLY PAPER I ever had a problem with was the *Daily Sport* though some may feel what happened was self-inflicted.

In 2000, Millwall chairman Theo Paphitis decided to charge players for toast at the training ground. His reasoning was, 'Every business I've got and every business I know has a subsidised canteen and working people pay for their food.

'On the money footballers earn they shouldn't be the exception, they should be the total opposite. They should be paying full price, not subsidised. Normal people pay for their food, so why not high-earning players? Anyway, they should be eating at home. I think we spoil them.'

When word got out, the *Daily Sport* decided it was a big story and sent a photographer and a rather attractive, red-haired female reporter wearing a long coat along to Millwall's training ground.

The club told the pair to go away, so they stood on the pavement outside and explained to several YTS boys, including myself, that they just wanted a photograph with some players holding a plate of toast.

Why not? The girl was fit.

I was 18 and along with a few others saw it as an opportunity for some fun press coverage. We agreed to pose for a picture, the girl already had a plate of toast which we were told to hold. We were then asked to smile and say 'cheese'. A second before the photographer's camera flashed – no pun intended – the girl's lovely brown coat dropped to the floor.

The 'reporter' was wearing only a thong. Apart from that, she was as naked as nature intended and certainly hotter than the toast. So there we were, in our Millwall kit, seven of us saying 'cheese' and suddenly a pair of 36DDs (my guess, not confirmed, though) appeared.

The photographer started to snap away. We thought it would be a photo and a caption that few would have seen. Wrong.

The next morning I received a text from a pal, 'Have you seen the *Daily Sport*?' I have never driven so quickly to the newsagent to buy a paper in my life. I flicked through the pages and there it was – centre-spread.

Fuck me, it's on two pages. But some say I have never had such a big grin on my face since.

The club went bonkers. We were called in to see Steve Gritt, the reserve team manager, who went apeshit. 'What the fuck were you thinking?' he asked.

No one answered.

A lesson was learned, just as it was when it cost me over £200 to realise that if you buy what you know is stolen property you can rightly pay the price.

When I was living in a flat my television packed in so I needed a new one. I was injured at the time and undergoing treatment in an oxygen chamber in Swanley. Coincidence or not, I was filling up my car in a garage and I couldn't believe my luck. A guy in a white van pulled up next to me and asked, 'Here mate, do you need a new TV?'

The television god was looking down on me.

He had a variety of widescreen plasma televisions, all the top brands in their boxes professionally and securely taped up. I wanted a Sony widescreen plasma and I was told it would cost £300. I had only £220 on me. 'That's okay,' he said albeit a little reluctantly and I helped him put the brand new boxed-up telly in the back of my car.

Or so I thought.

When I arrived home and opened the box, inside was not a state-of-the-art plasma television, but some battered old TV set probably picked up from a council dump. I had been done like a kipper and having helped him put it in my car made me feel even worse.

If I'm ever in Swanley again and a guy in a white van asks me if I want a TV I'll tell him to follow me to the furthest bank I can find and then drive off.

Sometimes in life you get what you deserve and that day I certainly did.

28

My best-ever Millwall XI

Muscat must be the skipper

I ALREADY know one of the most difficult tasks a manager faces – team selection. Not just choosing his first XI, but the dilemma of who to leave out.

As the fantasy Millwall manager I have chosen the best side of players with whom I played in the first team. It was not easy and plenty of good players were omitted.

Management. Bloody hell.

GOALKEEPER
DAVID FORDE
Millwall: 2008–
Millwall have had a tradition of outstanding goalkeepers over the past half-century. Bryan King (his 302 games is a club record for the position), Alex Stepney, Lawrie Leslie (whose

eight successive penalty saves, while not achieved at Millwall, was a world record), Kasey Keller, Brian Horne, more recently Tony Warner, Andy Marshall, Nigel Spink and Maik Taylor, but none showed true consistency over a few seasons.

The arrival of David Forde from Cardiff in 2008 changed that. It is not easy being a Millwall goalkeeper because the demands of the fans at The Den are high and audible, but Fordey had the character and mental strength not to let any outside influences trouble him.

I cannot remember another player whose passion to win surpasses Fordey's.

He helped to change and improve my game, making me a more solid defender by his sheer physical presence and personality. Fordey has controlled aggression during a match and when he comes out for a ball it's a safe bet he'll get it and woe betide any opposing forward – or team-mate – in his way.

Sometimes Fordey's aggression can get the better of him. At Watford, in October 2014, we were the victims of some inexplicable refereeing decisions and at half-time a very angry, frustrated Fordey ripped the visiting dressing-room door off its hinges.

Millwall, under Ian Holloway, had a policy, like the All Blacks, of always clearing their changing room on away trips. We left our Vicarage Road dressing room spick and span, just a pity about the door hanging off its hinges.

Succeeding Shay Given as the Republic of Ireland's regular goalkeeper helped Fordey become an ever better stopper. When he initially joined up with the Ireland squad he had a few self-doubts, wondering if he would be good enough at the highest level. It soon became apparent he was a goalkeeper of international stature and was the first choice in the latter days of Giovanni Trapattoni and when Martin O'Neill took over.

Fordey had played more games in the League of Ireland than in English football before he joined Millwall when he was 28 and that gave him a hunger and desire to succeed. Mission accomplished and he is by far the best keeper I have played with.

RIGHT-BACK
KEVIN MUSCAT
Millwall: 2003–05

Kevin Muscat's reputation will always overshadow how good a player he was, even if some of his tricks were borderline legal. Muscat was able to whistle and make it sound like the referee's whistle. How many hours he must have spent perfecting this dubious art I don't know, but it benefited Millwall on occasions.

Garry Flitcroft of Blackburn was clear on goal during one game and Muscat whistled. Flitcroft instinctively stopped, picked the ball up and threw it down in frustration, probably thinking he must have been offside. The referee said to him, 'What are you doing? I never blew.' He then awarded Millwall a free kick for Flitcroft's handball.

Eventually referees began to realise what Muscat was doing though he had to be caught in the act, which was not easy so he would still get away with it occasionally, usually when the opposing team had a free kick. I can remember some managers doing their nut in the technical area, but to punish Muzzy the referee had to be looking at him and witnessing his phantom whistling. Muzzy was very good at making sure it was not traceable.

Away from impersonating the referee's whistle, Muscat's tackling, his drive and a no-nonsense physical side made him what he was.

This may be difficult to believe, but off the pitch Muscat is one of the nicest people you could wish to meet.

On it, he was a natural born winner. I was his understudy and he was the right-back I hoped to be, inasmuch as I wanted his first-team place. Everyone feared Muscat and no one wanted to play against him. I, too, needed to have that edge against wingers because if I had some sort of reputation it would help me dominate opponents.

Subsequently this proved to be the case for me in a lot of big matches over the years. Muscat showed me how significant a part of the game intimidation is and though purists may call it one of football's darker arts, the beautiful game inevitably has a cutting edge, too.

I remember Muscat's first match for Millwall, away to Watford in 2003. Archie Knox, the assistant manager to Mark McGhee, told him, 'Nothing stupid today, Muzzy. We must keep everyone on the pitch.'

Within 45 minutes Muscat had been sent off after losing the plot big time when he stamped on Danny Webber. He also conceded a penalty and Watford went on to win 3-1.

Knox, who was also assistant to Sir Alex Ferguson at Aberdeen and Manchester United, was harder than nails and laid in to Muzzy afterwards, saying, 'You'll never fucking learn. I told you, nothing fucking stupid.' And that was the polite bit.

At his press conference, McGhee said, 'Insane is the only way to describe it. The ball was away and there was no danger, so to risk giving away a penalty and getting sent off is just plain crazy. It cost us the game. None of the other players defended him, which is unusual, because we all felt very let down.'

But that was typical Muzzy.

CENTRE-BACK
RICHARD SHAW
Millwall: 2006–08
Richard Shaw was an experienced professional when he joined Millwall, having played more than 500 matches for Crystal Palace and Coventry, but I never realised just how good he was until I played alongside him.

He read the game as well as anyone I've seen, he was exceptional. If you are not the quickest or the biggest you have to be one step ahead of everyone else and Shaw had this quality, which is why he played at the top level for so long.

Shaw was in the side at a time when Millwall were struggling under Willie Donachie in League 1, yet was named Player of the Year, just as he had been at Palace and Coventry. Despite the problems of the team, Shaw always stood out with his superb defending, his passing, marking ability, positional sense and awareness and, despite not being the tallest, his heading.

I thought he was a remarkable defender and it was a joy and privilege to play with him.

Shaw tried his hand at coaching with Millwall and then at Coventry where he was assistant manager. I don't think he had the mean streak that a lot of managers have.

He was almost too nice, a gentleman, there wasn't a nasty bone in his body which in football is not necessarily an advantage.

CENTRE-BACK
SEAN DYCHE

Millwall: 1999–2002

Not Rhino? No, because he was finishing his long and distinguished playing career as mine was starting, though we played together in the reserves a few times.

During one such game against Luton, the ball bounced between us and he shouted 'Rhino's' but it was too late. I was committed to the clearance and could not stop my momentum. If that wasn't bad enough, the ball hit him smack in the face.

If looks could kill I would not be here now.

I immediately said, 'Sorry, gaffer.' There was no bollocking from Rhino who simply ordered me to 'fucking get back' because the game was in progress.

While Rhino was a one-club man, Sean Dyche had played most of his career with Chesterfield and as much as he was a calm, composed defender, he could also talk for England. He could chat about a Mars bar for three days. Dyche loved his food and was always telling us about his cooking though as a young player I must confess it was a subject that did not hold my interest.

On the field, Dyche's ability to talk – or shout – was an asset. Able to play as either a left- or right-side central defender, he was more of a stopper centre-half than Richard Shaw. Dyche was always totally professional and did his job in a quietly effective way.

When you play with someone you tend not to think whether he will go on to be a successful coach or manager. You tend to just concentrate on playing and let any subsequent career take care of itself.

Dyche helped Millwall to win promotion to Division One in 2001 and we then came close to securing a Premier League place the following year, but lost to eventual promotion winners Birmingham City in the play-offs.

He went on to manage Watford before guiding Burnley back to the Premier League in 2014 and the man who could talk for England has become a media favourite because of this skill.

LEFT-BACK
TONY CRAIG
Millwall: 2003–07; 2008–12; 2015–
This was the most difficult position to fill because it is a long time since Millwall had a left-back who has dominated the position. I chose Tony Craig who joined Millwall for the third time in 2015, and will be honoured with a well-deserved testimonial.

I remember Tony in one of his first reserve matches and I could see his passion for the game then. Not many players wear shin pads in the warm-up. He was a young boy with old-school shin pads and socks pulled up.

I thought to myself, 'He's keen.'

Tony was a quiet lad, but as soon as he stepped on the pitch he was a different person, immediately showing the Millwall spirit.

A good pro, a good honest player, Tony is someone you need in the dressing room.

He has always been a solid, consistent performer who can play left- centre-half or left-back. Tony's spirit and versatility wins him a place in my starting XI.

RIGHT-MIDFIELD
JASON PUNCHEON
Millwall: November 2010–January 2011

Jason Puncheon spent ten weeks on loan to Millwall from Southampton where he had lost his place to Alex Oxlade-Chamberlain.

I believe the hat-trick he scored against Crystal Palace at The Den, on New Year's Day 2011, ended his chances of joining Millwall on a permanent basis.

Millwall's 3-0 victory also cost Palace manager George Burley his job as he was sacked an hour after the final whistle.

As I tended to be suspended every time Millwall played Palace, I watched the game from the stand. After Puncheon had scored his second goal I said to myself, 'Get him off now. If he scores a hat-trick there will be headlines and his value will go up.'

I knew Millwall were keen to sign Puncheon on a permanent basis but when he completed his hat-trick his value soared to £1m-plus.

He was eventually replaced by James Henry with six minutes remaining though by then it was too late. The financial damage had been done and he was out of Millwall's price range.

Puncheon is similar to me in that he can be a bit of a hot-head. He's a street kid from Croydon and it was a slow climb up the football ladder via Wimbledon, Milton Keynes Dons, Fisher, Lewes, Barnet and Plymouth before joining Southampton and in 2014 signing for Crystal Palace.

He has no fear on the ball, is extremely skilful with a wonderful left foot and he can play on either wing. A tricky player, Puncheon scored five goals in his seven games for

Millwall, but they were enough to convince me that he was a special player.

It was no surprise when he played a significant part in Palace's remarkable recovery in 2013/14 after they had looked certs for relegation from the Premier League.

CENTRE-MIDFIELD
TIM CAHILL

Millwall: 1998–2004

Tim Cahill came over from Australia when Millwall signed him on a free transfer from Sydney United. Even as a teenager it was obvious that he was a very talented player. Of all his attributes, his heading and hang-time in the air are the most well known. We used to call him 'kangaroo' because of the way he could leap.

Despite being only 5ft 10in, Cahill went on to break the Premier League record of headed goals with his 27th such effort, ahead of specialists such as Dion Dublin, Duncan Ferguson and Les Ferdinand.

Apart from having this unlikely heading ability for someone relatively small, I often wonder if Cahill was blessed in other ways, too. Whatever he did, he would win. If he picked an outsider in the Grand National sweepstake his horse would come first; if he played darts or snooker he would get the crucial double top or make the highest break. He was not a popular cards opponent, I can tell you.

On the pitch he was always in the right place at the right time, not least to notch the winner – with his foot – in the 2004 FA Cup semi-final against Sunderland. Cahill seemed to score important goals rather than the third in a 3-0 win which made him so valuable. From free kicks and corners he was almost impossible to mark because he had a knack of finding a gap as the ball came in.

He left Millwall in the summer of 2004 and at £1.5m Everton picked up one of the finest bargains in Premier League history.

He scored 108 goals for Millwall and Everton, more than half with his head, before moving to Major League Soccer and the New York Red Bulls in 2012. Like Frank Lampard, Cahill could virtually guarantee you 15 goals a season, a terrific return from a midfielder. Unlike Lampard, Cahill rarely took penalties.

Not only did he score regularly for Millwall and Everton, Cahill became Australia's all-time record goalscorer. His sensational volley against Holland at the 2014 World Cup finals was, for me, the best goal of the tournament and there were plenty of outstanding candidates to choose from. To hit the ball on the volley as perfectly as he did when the ball came to him is the hardest skill in football.

Cahill has gone on to become a multi-millionaire and good luck to him. They loved him in New York where he has become a brand, with companies such as adidas, FIFA, Gatorade and Weetabix using him, while he has his own soccer schools. I'm sure he's as popular in China with Shanghai Shenhua. He is proof that nice guys can finish first.

Mind you, this didn't prevent him from wrecking my flat in Bromley one Christmas.

With some Christmas spirit taken on board, it became the silly season with Cahill thinking it would be a good idea to remove chicken wings from the fridge and put them in my shoes. When he ran out of chicken, he turned to filling the remaining shoes with shampoo. Then, he took the decorations off the Christmas tree and used some of them as would-be footballs.

When I confronted him, he said in his unmistakable Aussie accent, 'Wasn't me, mate.'

CENTRE-MIDFIELD
DENNIS WISE
Millwall: 2002–05

I was fortunate to play with Dennis Wise who, like Kevin Muscat, often had his ability overlooked because of some disciplinary excesses. Wise was an extremely clever player on the ball and to be that small – 5ft 6in – and play for Chelsea for 11 years is no mean feat.

Yes, he was a little terror, at times bordering on nasty, who demanded the absolute best from everyone. Losing was a personal insult for Wisey who was loved by the Millwall fans for the way he could win the ball from someone much bigger than he was – one way or the other.

His precision passing, either from set pieces or open play, was an object lesson to players young and old. Wise was nearing the end of his playing career when he joined Millwall initially as a player and then becoming player-manager, but even in his mid-30s Wise's quality shone through. He was never the fastest so didn't have much pace to lose, but his natural ability still put him head and shoulders above the rest.

LEFT-MIDFIELD
ANDROS TOWNSEND
Millwall: March 2011–May 2011

It was no surprise that Andros Townsend went on to make such a promising impact for England in 2013, an injury spoiling his chances of being part of their Brazil 2014 squad. His injury was untimely – he could have given England something extra at the World Cup because of how direct he is – and jeez, did they need it.

I have never seen such professionalism in one so young. He was 20 when he joined us on loan from Spurs – Millwall were the sixth club he had been loaned to.

Townsend was a quiet lad who put everything he could into training. He had a mean streak in him, no bad thing, and was not slow in reacting if things did not go his way, which is unusual for a youngster.

When he finished training he would be first into the ice bath to prepare for the exertions ahead. Townsend wasn't interested in anything outside of football, he didn't really join in the dressing-room jokes or any socialising. He would holiday with his family rather than go on vacation with mates.

He knew what he was doing, which path he was taking because his talent was phenomenal. I know that because when he was on loan to Yeovil I was sent off for two yellow card offences against him – trying to win the ball that, because of his speed, wasn't there. For a full-back, the most challenging aspect of facing a winger is when he has genuine pace which Townsend does. He should not take it too much as a criticism when I say he is not quite as fast as Gareth Bale – few are – but having been on the receiving end of Townsend's pace I know how difficult it is to mark him.

Townsend was equally effective with his left or right foot and was one of a number of Spurs players who benefited from a loan period with Millwall.

In his short spell at The Den, I saw Townsend destroy teams.

We'd give him the ball and let him run at opposing defences because we knew nine times out of ten he would deliver the cross.

STRIKER
HARRY KANE
Millwall: December 2011–May 2012

Harry Kane joined Millwall on loan from Tottenham with Ryan Mason. Three years later they were established members of the Spurs first team.

At Millwall, Kane played alongside Darius Henderson in attack and while his ability was obvious I never thought he would soon be one of the Premier League's leading strikers. He did, however, score the best goal I have ever seen, albeit in a training game.

The goalkeeper threw the ball to Kane who flicked it over his marker's head before scoring with a stunning volley from the narrowest of angles. The only goal I can compare it with is Marco van Basten's Euro 88 strike for Holland against the Soviet Union.

Kane's seven goals in 22 appearances for Millwall went a long way to helping us stay in the Championship and earned the then 18-year-old the Young Player of the Year award. In fact, Millwall didn't lose any of the games in which he scored.

He was a quiet lad, very genuine and credit to Tottenham for the way he has progressed.

Kane has gone on to become one of the Premier League's leading strikers, establishing himself in the England team, but it is good that he never forgot what he regards as an important part of his learning curve at Millwall.

Kane scored the winner against Portsmouth which secured Millwall's place in the Championship. 'I'll never forget it,' he told the *Evening Standard*. 'The relief on everyone's faces – the players, the fans. It showed me how much the game could mean. People were playing for their livelihoods and had they been relegated, it would have been a big downer for the club.

'You have to do your job otherwise you won't be in the game long so to be thrown into that at 18 was really good. That experience [with Millwall] is one of the things that have made me who I am today.'

STRIKER
NEIL HARRIS
Millwall: 1998–2004; 2007–11

I have known Neil Harris for more than half of my life and he is someone I would class not just as a Millwall legend, but also someone who has been very helpful, giving me plenty of good advice about the bad things I was doing as a teenager.

In January 2009, Harris broke Teddy Sheringham's all-time goalscoring record for Millwall during the 3-2 away win against Crewe Alexandra with his 112th goal for the club. This guaranteed him iconic status at The Den.

His relationship and chemistry with the Millwall fans was exceptional. He deserved their total support because of the dedication he put in, not only during training, but afterwards, too. The older Harris was, the harder he worked.

A two-footed striker, he didn't have great pace, but always got into the right areas and had a cut-back trick defenders always fell for, pulling the ball back before shooting.

After training, he would stay behind to practise finishing, another player sending the ball over so he could strike it on the volley or control it with one touch and shoot with the next. I do not see today's generation putting in such extra work.

Harris was devastated when he had to pull down the curtain on his playing days – it happens to us all one day – but he could look back on a wonderful career. Harris started coaching at Millwall with the under-21s before succeeding Ian Holloway in March 2015 and I believe he will become a top-class manager one day.

CAPTAIN
KEVIN MUSCAT

Choosing the captain was almost harder than selecting the team. He should be someone who leads by example, has a will to win, a hunger to succeed, is a good talker and reads the game well.

While Kevin Muscat's disciplinary record is hardly the best, he showed as Millwall captain that he had leadership qualities that inspired his team-mates. He would run through a brick wall to reach the ball. There are many spoofers in football, players who kid you about how good they are, but the former Australia captain is the real deal.

Muzzy gets the armband.

29

Football banter
can be fun

If it doesn't become intimidating

BANTER – an exchange of light, playful, teasing remarks; good-natured raillery. The dictionary's definition of 'banter' is rather different to the 'playful' fun that is part and parcel of every dressing room. To those not involved in the game, football banter may be another way of saying bullying and I admit that at times the line in the sand can be crossed. I was the victim of bullying when I was younger and I hate to see anyone taken advantage of in such an unacceptable manner.

Yet footballers live in a different world in some ways and if you ask any ex-player what he misses most after he retires, he will almost certainly say it is the dressing-room banter.

Every day I live for banter, for a laugh and for fun, but when it reaches a stage where someone is belittled and feels uncomfortable, especially if more than one person is picking on him, then banter can become bullying.

Earlier in my career I remember the older players bantering the YTS scholars to such a degree where it became intimidating. That is taking it too far. It could be remarks about clothes, anything really, and it affected my confidence.

In the hierarchy of football, a YTS could not really bite back to a senior pro in those days, though thankfully, things have changed.

The banter is nowhere near as bad as it was 15 or 20 years ago, while younger players are able to stick up for themselves more readily.

*　*　*　*　*

I THINK it's important to be able to take the piss out of yourself because if you can't do that, you shouldn't do it to others. Too many can give it but not take it.

Yes, I've been guilty of going over the top with 'jokes' which I regret, but the times when banter is pushed too far is invariably fuelled by booze and then it can all kick off. I've seen players slap a team-mate across the face, saying, 'Pass it on.'

It is not a game anyone should try and neither is what happened at a Millwall Christmas party in Chinawhite nightclub when one of the lads brought a boxing glove along. The idea was, if you were caught drinking with your right hand you received a left-hander from someone with the boxing glove. Then you put the glove on to wait for the next wrong-handed drinker.

It was probably not the best idea and certainly wasn't when, inevitably, it was taken too far and the sight of a player wearing a boxing glove chasing a team-mate round the nightclub must have made the other revellers wonder what the fuck was happening.

During our pre-season in Portugal before the start of 2014/15 we were allowed a night out with a midnight curfew. As the new captain, Ian Holloway put me in charge of ensuring everyone was back at the hotel by 12.

'Yes, gaffer.'

We had four hours to sample the delights of Albufeira before the coach left at 11 and we started with pub golf which was Josh Wright's idea. Drinks are rated as a par five down to a par one which means if, say, you have a pint it would be a par five so you have five 'gulps' to finish it.

I was trying to be sensible and in golf terms I probably triple-bogeyed every drink. I kept to the manager's order to make sure everyone was on the coach by 11 to be home by 12.

That was the hardest bit done – or so I thought. Twenty lads, all safe and sound on the coach. Sorted. What could go wrong?

Apart from the Portuguese police being called, one player hit for taking a piss in the wrong place and being 90 minutes late, very little.

As we boarded the coach Jermaine Easter decided it would be fun to 'playfully' slap Martin Woolford on the back of his head and Scott McDonald thought it overstepped the banter mark. Things went from bad to worse and Easter and McDonald had a blazing row with the pair coming to blows.

We told Easter to sit at the front and McDonald to go to the back, but the verbals between the pair became so loud and abusive the driver threatened to call the police. Things quietened down for a while until some of the players, who had enjoyed their share of par ones, started to bang on the windows shouting, 'We want McDonald's, we want McDonald's.'

Not Scott, but burgers.

The driver had heard enough. He pulled into a petrol station in the middle of nowhere and carried through his threat to call the police, who turned out to be armed police.

They lined us all up in a row by the side of the road where we had to sit down like naughty schoolkids. We had to give them our names one by one – I think I may have given them an incorrect surname, so it was only half a lie.

John Marquis wanted a piss so asked a policeman where he could go. Because of the language problems, Marquis didn't know the policeman was telling him there was a toilet round the back and instead had a jimmy riddle in a bush – halfway through it one of the coppers hit him across the back of his legs because he was pissing in a hedge.

It was 11.30pm when the police arrived and all they wanted to do was inconvenience us. We got back to the hotel at half past one – 90 minutes late.

Not a great start as captain of Millwall.

I told the gaffer we missed the curfew by an hour and a half – needless to say he already knew – and when the next training session started at 7.30am the following day – yes, 7.30am – things weren't so funny after all. The manager asked the squad, 'Who was late?' and everyone owned up. While the instigators were Easter and McDonald, the squad stuck together and we all suffered.

The gaffer ran the bollocks off us, up and down hills. I was livid because I remained relatively sober, got all the lads on the coach on time, but had still let the manager down.

You could say what happened that night pushed the boundaries of banter too far, but I still think the word is appropriate in a dressing-room context.

What else do we say? Fun? Japes? Hijinks?

30

Coaching and management beckons

I want to play until no one wants me

Alan Dunne – Millwall Manager

ONE DAY, maybe, just maybe, this will become reality. My long-term ambition is to become a manager and when I cast my mind forward to a career after playing, managing Millwall inevitably runs through my head.

The worry I have about this is that most managerial jobs have a swift and unhappy ending. With the average tenure of a manager in the lower divisions lasting less than a season, the odds on the sack are short. Very short. Statistics published in 2015 revealed that 40 per cent of managers do not reach 75 games in charge.

However, this is a concern for the future.

My love of the game will always push me towards playing until no one wants me because a footballer is a long time retired.

✳   ✳   ✳   ✳   ✳

THE KNEE injury sustained by Carlos Edwards making a routine tackle in September 2014, which left the experienced right-back looking at a year of recovery, underlined that we are all one challenge away from seeing our careers potentially being ended.

Players tend to take it for granted that they will finish playing when old age tells them it is time to hang up their boots. It is on our minds all the time, but we assume a career-ending injury is something that happens to someone else.

In my first four months at Leyton Orient I witnessed two anterior cruciate ligament injuries – both non-contact – to Dean Cox and Paul McCallum. These injuries mean a minimum of six to nine months of rehabilitation and are becoming more common. Perhaps it's because of the sort of boots we wear, or the grass that clubs favour. There is a study going on to discover if there is a common link in any ACL injuries. Of course, it could just be a case of bad luck.

Danny Senda was never the same after snapping an Achilles tendon against Swindon in May 2008 which caused him to be on the sidelines for 16 months. Joe Dolan broke his left leg in 2001 and then tore a cruciate ligament in his comeback though he went on to play non-league football for almost ten years.

If you are in the last year of your contract a long-term injury has an even bigger impact.

You may have only eight pay packets remaining and as businesses, clubs are not going to do you any favours by offering you a new deal with your future in doubt.

This is why players are keen to tie down long-term contracts because it gives them more security, especially when the big 3-0 approaches or has even passed. When you are younger you have more chance of recovering from a bad injury and finding another club. The older you are the more difficult this can be.

While being injured is always a worry for every player, the more you think about it the easier it can be for something nasty to happen. You have to train with intensity because if you don't you are more likely to be hurt.

Injuries are part of your journey as a footballer, whichever level you play. I saw Edwards a couple of days after he did his knee and told him how gutted I was for him. But there is no point in being all doom and gloom, even to a team-mate who is looking at a year on the sidelines.

I told him to get a new PlayStation 5, a lazy chair and a decent headset to help him pass the time on his long haul back to fitness.

Touch wood, I have never had a prolonged spell out of the game. My worst injury was probably to the scaphoid bone on my right hand. I broke it when I was pushed into the dug-out during a game against Burnley at The Den.

The wrist was in a cast for eight weeks, but compared to what some players have been through I have been lucky.

✳   ✳   ✳   ✳   ✳

MY AMBITION is to become a coach and then have a crack at management. I think ideally you need to have had five or six years' coaching experience before becoming a manager.

I have completed my UEFA B Licence which enables me to coach outside the Premier League and Championship. The UEFA A Licence course is done over two years and I started it during the summer of 2015.

The highest qualification is the UEFA Pro Licence, which takes 18 months to complete, and is required by anyone who wishes to manage a football club in the top level of the nation's league system on a permanent basis.

One of the biggest challenges for a player when his career ends is how he reacts to the change of routine and, if he was lucky enough to be in the public spotlight, how he handles no longer being a centre of attention.

The buzz and adrenalin rush you had from being a player suddenly vanishes.

Neil Harris coached Millwall's under-21s before his promotion to the senior team in March 2015. Coaching under-age sides is an important job within a club but is a far cry from playing against some of the biggest teams in England and sharing the dressing-room banter with familiar faces.

This is part of the learning process for a coach, to make the switch from being a player and there is no point looking back over the good old days. You must concentrate on helping the next generation in their bid for glory.

From earning decent money as a player, a rookie coach has to take a significant drop in wages. Life after playing is a worry for all players and planning for the dreaded R-day is important.

In most jobs you retire at 65; a footballer is fortunate if he makes it to 35.

Footballers never do anything else but play football. For 20 years or so it is the only thing they have done. This is why, when I was 30, I turned my attention to completing my UEFA coaching courses to start preparing for life after playing the beautiful game.

Some believe it is best to start your coaching or managerial career with a lower league club, but I think you should aim for the club highest in the English football structure who wants you. It is like being a player. If you sign your first pro contract with a Premier League club, you will find another club relatively easily if things do not work out because of the better coaching you have had.

If you manage a big club and leave, you should still find alternative employment whereas being sacked by a League 2 outfit is likely to see you struggle for another job.

❊   ❊   ❊   ❊   ❊

SO HOW would Alan Dunne the manager handle an Alan Dunne-type player?

First of all, wish him luck.

He would have to understand him. Kenny Jackett is the best manager I have worked under, but initially he could not work me out though Ian Holloway did very quickly.

Even as a young boy I was a bit of a problem player with youth team managers having to keep an eye on me. I was the one who missed the coach or had a fight on the training ground. I've never been frightened of anyone and while I was a good player, I was not the easiest to handle.

A week before I was due to sign my first pro contract one of the schoolboys nicked my Jaffa Cakes – he was probably

14, three years younger than me. I think I headbutted him. No, I did headbutt him. One of the other players grassed me to Kevin O'Callaghan, the youth team manager.

I was called into his office and Bob Pearson, who was in charge of pro contracts, told me that the deal I was about to sign was suspended 'until further notice'.

Talk about stupidity.

I was fined a week's wages – £45 – and told that every afternoon I had to be on the pitch with the Millwall youth team physio Colin Clifford – by God do I owe this guy. O'Callaghan told him I had to do six pitch laps in a certain time and for every one when I didn't make the time, I had to do another.

I don't think I beat the clock once, but each time I crossed the line Clifford would shout, 'Well done, Dunney, just made it.'

O'Callaghan was looking from his office to make sure I wasn't cheating. I had to do this every day for a week and 'just made it' each time. If only he knew.

A month later I eventually signed my first pro contract and my mum and dad took me to McDonald's to celebrate. And they paid.

To walk away from The Den and be able to call myself a professional footballer was all I ever dreamed of as a kid.

✳   ✳   ✳   ✳   ✳

I GAVE my managers something to think about, probably playing up to this image at times. I liked to be different. I don't think managers mind this too much, as long as it's not excessive.

I have always been at my best when I am not being praised. Whenever a manager has started to blow smoke up my arse I tended to get carried away with it. I started to take things for granted and my form suffered.

What I hope no manager – or indeed, anybody – can doubt is that I have always given 100 per cent for the shirt regardless of what else may be going on. I have also never been one to go knocking on the gaffer's door to ask why I wasn't playing. Players tend to know why they have been left out, even if they do not want to admit it.

I have never wanted a manager to like me. I feel uncomfortable if someone is constantly giving me credit because I lose my edge. There is something about this that I don't think is right though on the other hand everyone likes to be praised.

I want to hear it, but I don't.

Jackett eventually worked me out and never told me that I'd had a good game, no matter how well I'd played. When I was chosen as Millwall's Player of the Year and won the Goal of the Season trophy he congratulated me, but added, 'If anyone tells you that you are a really good player don't believe them. If someone tells you that you are crap don't believe them either.'

That was clever man-management. A word of praise, but with a warning not to get carried away.

As I have become older, I have understood managers more, able to see things from their perspective. Some players never take their blinkers off and assume everyone they play for is a wanker and they know more than the boss. I have tried to put myself into the manager's shoes, wondering how he is thinking and what he has to do.

263

I hope that what I have learned during my playing days will serve me well in the next step of my career. I haven't had my eyes closed as a player and I have so many ideas I cannot wait to put into practice as a coach or manager.

The game is forever changing and I am not sure if all managers – or players – are keeping up with this. What worked five or six years ago doesn't necessarily work now. Managers need to have different formations they can use because sticking to one plan will not bring success.

You need to be flexible during a game. If Plan A isn't working, try Plan B – don't just bring on subs and stay with Plan A.

Scouting reports and the use of computers mean all teams are better prepared than ever, so any weakness in the opposition can be exploited. This means you must be able to adapt your formation or tactics to win the match.

Holloway took it to an extreme, trying to teach us how the great Barcelona team won games. The philosophy may be good but it was difficult to transfer this to our level. On the other hand, Mick McCarthy knows how to win Championship matches, using his own methods to positive effect.

If I am handed the chance to show what I can do, I will not be a 'safe' or basic manager, someone who is so scared of losing.

No one wants to be defeated, but I would rather be more adventurous and hopefully entertaining and take what results come our way.

31

I can tell if a player is good enough in five minutes

A strong handshake is also a must

I T TAKES me about five minutes to size up a player, be it a kid promoted to the first-team squad or a new signing. I can tell by their demeanour, their attitude, how good their first or second touch is, by their first pass. I can get a pretty good idea from this. I've found it is rare that my initial opinion is wrong.

Of course, there is an exception to every rule. Berry Powel, a Dutch player Millwall signed from Den Bosch in 2005, had not even trained with us, but scored two minutes into his debut against Cardiff to earn us a draw.

That was as good as it got for Powel – it was his first and last goal for Millwall. He lasted only 12 matches and his form prompted one fans' website to say, 'He couldn't score in a brothel.'

While everyone can have an off day, whether he is with a Premier League club or a League 2 team, a player must show the hunger, commitment and determination plus, of course, the technique that will make the manager think he deserves a new contract.

The biggest mistake a manager can make is to show any weakness from the day he walks in. If he does, then it will be an uphill struggle. He has to immediately instil a fear inside his players. Fear and respect are different emotions – players tend to respect the guy who walks through the door more often than not because he's earned the job.

Fear is knowing the manager is in charge, don't mess with him because if he has the backing of the chairman it puts him in a position of strength.

A weakness can show itself in different ways. A manager should not be high-profile every day at the training ground where his assistant can take charge. Kenny Jackett would rarely be seen on a Monday or Tuesday, but come Thursday and Friday he was preparing the team for the match on Saturday.

You need a coach with a strong personality who the players know they cannot take advantage of because the boss is elsewhere. Behind every good manager is a good coach.

There must also be a line in the sand which the manager cannot cross. He is not able to join in the banter with the players one minute and then front a team meeting the next. A manager has to be totally professional seven days a week and that does not include socialising or laughing and joking with his players like he's one of the boys.

I can tell if a player is good enough in five minutes

It is essential for the man in charge to be positive at all times, however the side is playing. Jackett and Ian Holloway had this quality, a desire that comes across to the squad at all times. A manager's job means his family may have to take second place as he watches future opponents or possible new signings.

And unlike players, the boss tends not to go home after training.

GIVEN MY disciplinary record, I know as a manager I will leave myself open to criticism by clamping down on players who step out of line. However, every club needs a code of conduct and a fines system in place (at Millwall I was sometimes the biggest donor).

Being late is not acceptable, though with a training-ground bust-up or even a red card I would look at each case individually. Unless the sending-off was for something really stupid I would probably show some understanding because I've been there, seen it and done it.

A mistimed tackle or a non-violent push on an opponent could not be treated in the same way as an elbow to the face.

One thing that cannot be justified is dissent. This is something I have rarely been booked for, whereas my mate Barry Hayles was constantly cautioned for giving his opinion to referees.

It would be very difficult for me to back a player who has argued with the referee or an assistant. That can be controlled even in the heat of the battle and refs never change their minds just because a player disagrees with his decision.

Apart from the way the game is played, how players look has also changed. I know Manchester United insist on their players wearing a club suit, shirt and tie before and after games, though I believe tracksuits are equally acceptable.

Players would not feel comfortable driving ten miles (or in or around London, for an hour) in a shirt and tie. As someone who is now on first-name terms with the Blackwall Tunnel since joining Leyton Orient, I feel more comfortable sitting in the inevitable traffic jam in a tracksuit rather than a lounge suit.

When we reached Wembley for the League 1 Play-Off Final against Scunthorpe United we had club suits and we were almost so fixated on looking good we took our eye off the game, which we lost.

The following year when we played Swindon we wore tracksuits, felt more relaxed and won.

✳ ✳ ✳ ✳ ✳

WE LIVE in the age of the mobile phone which has taken over some people's lives. Texting and being on social media is something we have to accept, if not totally agree with.

Footballers are forever on their phones. As soon as they come off the training pitch, away they go texting to anyone and everyone and discovering important world matters like what their girlfriend is doing. It's an addiction.

On matchdays I would ban them from the dressing room after the team meeting at 1.30pm. Following that, phones should be switched off with players concentrating on the forthcoming game.

They would have their excuses like sorting out tickets, or dad wanting to know if he is playing, but after half past one I would not want to see a phone until half past five when players are leaving the dressing room.

ONE ASPECT that will probably never change in English football is what the manager is called (to his face, anyway). Boss or gaffer are set in stone and I'd be happy with either one.

I guess football is the only profession where your boss is actually called boss, but there has to be a status where the manager is above the players. I think it is respectful, although Ian Holloway didn't mind being called Ollie and Neil Harris is happy to be called Neil.

Maybe if the older lads called me Dunney I wouldn't object, but with younger players it would have to be boss.

Something I would insist on is a good, firm handshake which I have mentioned elsewhere in the book. If a player comes to sign I would not want to shake hands with a wet fish.

I'd see an immediate weakness in him and excuse me if this sounds a little sexist, but I want players to shake my hand like a man.

IT IS impossible to underestimate the value of team spirit to a club's success. I have been part of Millwall sides where the togetherness has been terrific – sadly, I also experienced the negative effects of an unhappy dressing room.

If everyone is pulling for each other, team spirit can win matches. Similarly, if there are different factions in the side it can cost you points.

Of course, it is unrealistic to expect 20 or so guys from different backgrounds to all get on and like each other. Andrew Cole and Teddy Sheringham were not on each other's Christmas card list yet this did not stop Manchester United winning the Treble in 1999 and more.

United still had a team spirit, a willingness for everyone to do anything for the team, a collective drive that saw them dominate English football.

In the lower leagues such camaraderie and closeness can be equally effective. A team wins together and loses together. A will to win can be more crucial than a skill to win.

Dennis Wise was the king of the bonding nights. He would invite not only the players, but wives or partners to a restaurant in London. Wisey once asked each girl to stand up and say something about her partner in ten seconds. Before we were married, Aimee said, 'He's still not asked me yet.'

I soon got the hint.

It was great fun and made for an unbelievable team spirit where not just the players, but also the girls felt part of a really good thing.

This was a major factor in the success we had under Wisey.

32

A creep from Crawley made me see red

Orient are the ideal springboard for the next stage of my career

IT WAS my second League 2 start for Leyton Orient. Though Crawley were beating us 2-1 we were playing well and I was comfortable with the way things were going for me in the centre of defence.

Thirty seconds before half-time Rhys Murphy and I chased a ball in our penalty area. I tried to anticipate him diving and put the brakes on because any touch and he'd go down.

I was right. He did.

I never touched him. Maybe he clipped his own foot, but down he went. Kevin Wright, the referee, was behind me and could not see there was no contact and if I may have a little sympathy for him awarding a penalty, the ball was not going directly towards goal which I thought meant it was not an obvious denial of a goalscoring opportunity. Either way, the red card was shown and Crawley scored from the penalty.

I felt I had let the players, the manager and the fans down which really hurt me. When the lads came in at half-time I was just sitting there with my head in my hands feeling awful. As someone once said – why always me?

Nobody said anything because everyone had to concentrate on the game, which we ultimately lost 3-2. I was praying we'd get at least a draw because then what had happened would not be so costly, but it was not to be.

I apologised to the other players, telling them I hadn't touched Murphy. Manager Ian Hendon was supportive of me, saying to the press, 'I don't think it should have been a sending-off. If you look closely at the video, the lad was already on his way down before Dunney got anywhere near him.'

Me, I was still livid and in true Dunne style I tried to see the referee.

✻   ✻   ✻   ✻   ✻

I KNOCKED on the match officials' room after the game – I knew I wasn't supposed to do that – and the ref shouted, 'Is that Martin?'

I said, 'Yes,' whoever Martin was.

The ref said, 'I'll be five minutes.'

As I was waiting outside, assistant manager Andy Hessenthaler and assistant coach Kevin Nugent got wind of what was happening. Before they arrived one of the Orient backroom team showed me the incident on his laptop several times and you could not see any contact between me and Rhys Murphy.

Andy and Kevin told me they would see the referee, who I felt owed me an apology. With the red mist in me still present, I asked a Crawley player if he could 'get the lad who I supposedly fouled, I want to see him'. I think he sussed it was not to exchange shirts.

Murphy came out bare-chested and instead of shirts, insults were exchanged though I kept saying to myself, 'Be calm, be calm.' The old me would have ripped his nose off.

'Did I touch you at any point?'

'Yeh, yeh you touched me.'

'I've looked on the laptop and I didn't.'

'Course you did, course you did.'

Andy joined in. 'No he didn't touch you, you went down before he touched you.'

Murphy and Andy became involved in a less-than-friendly argument and I could feel the time bomb in my brain ticking.

Thankfully, it didn't go off.

'Take a breath Alan, take a breath.'

I walked just inside the Crawley dressing room when their manager Mark Yates came in.

'What are you doing? Get away from our changing room.'

'Murphy came out to us, we didn't go in and get him.'

'Fuck off, get away.'

'Why are you getting angry?'

Things escalated.

'Don't do anything stupid Alan. You're at an away ground.'

I was dragged away while Yates's players pulled him back in the room.

Red card number 11. In the cold light of day I accepted that while against the spirit of the game, diving is part of football, especially when you get away with it.

✳ ✳ ✳ ✳ ✳

I TOLD Ian Hendon I was here to help the club win promotion, whether I was in the starting XI or a sub.

I joined Orient five weeks into their pre-season which meant I had a fair bit of catching up to do. The team started the season well, winning the first five games, so this, coupled with my lack of sharpness and match fitness, made it almost impossible for the manager to put me straight in the side.

At 33, Orient are the ideal club for me, a springboard for the next stage of my career. I am enjoying watching how things work at a different club...a different set-up...different managers and coaches with different ideas.

Importantly for me, I am learning all the time.

I am not at Orient to try to be in the team week-in, week-out. While any player wants to play in every match, I am doing all I can to help my team-mates all the time. I have not been sitting on the bench with my eyes shut picking up my money. I like to think I have been a good pro on the training pitch, contributing all I can, saying the right things and giving advice to those around me.

There aren't many players with a big ego at Orient. In fact, I can't think of any. We have a good, honest team who work hard for each other.

They ask me each week, 'Any idea who Millwall are playing?'

As if I didn't know.

'Stop talking about Millwall, Dunney.'

'You asked me a question.'

All banter and fun.

✳   ✳   ✳   ✳   ✳

I DIDN'T make the best of starts to my career with the O's. Three penalties conceded in four games and one red card.

The move from Millwall proved more difficult that I thought it would be. The expectation, the travelling and the training load, which is harder than what I'd been used to, were not easy to adjust to.

Our televised match at Hartlepool in November 2015 was a chance for me to show the Leyton Orient fans what I could really do. But I fucked up.

With Orient leading 1-0 and cruising, when Hartlepool's first cross of the game came over I was sandwiched between two players. Attempting to block the first man and hold down the second, my left arm was raised and the ball struck it. Penalty and 1-1.

We continued to dominate the match, going in at half-time confident we could win. Despite having more possession than Hartlepool, we lost 3-1.

It was a nightmare for me. Apart from the penalty, their second goal took a deflection off me. From a personal viewpoint the game could hardly have gone worse.

Ian Hendon rightly grilled me after the match in the dressing room. 'Dunney, you've given another penalty away, you've cost me three penalties, you're a Championship defender and I expect better from you.'

There was no argument from me. I just apologised.

It was probably the least pleasant journey back ever. About 45 minutes after we had left Victoria Park, the manager came down the back of the coach. 'Boys...the president [Francesco Becchetti] wants us to stay in a hotel tonight and for the rest of the week so we can assess our current slump in results.,

While this caused inconvenience to the players, we all realised that something needed to be done to turn things around. Inevitably this gained huge media coverage though despite the headlines it was not a punishment. The players bought into it and at the cost to the president we spent four nights together as a team – players and staff – in a top hotel eating excellent food.

The time was used to evaluate our game and work on what we needed to put right for the next game at home to York City. We were allowed home on Thursday and six days after I had left for Hartlepool it was wonderful to be with Aimee, Lola, Shay and Louis again.

Perhaps unsurprisingly, I was on the bench for the game and while a 3-2 victory over a team one point above the relegation zone may not sound convincing, we won. This match was always going to be about the result and victory was crucial as nearly all the sides above us won.

Despite the victory over York, results did not pick up... we had too many draws and far too many goals conceded. I sat for 12 games without a sniff of getting on – rightly or wrongly Hendon did not trust me to play because of my bad start. I went to see the manager three matches before he was sacked and asked him to give me another chance as I felt my experience could help him and the team.

Hendon appreciated me seeing him and said he was considering recalling me, but he was finding this very difficult. Maybe he was worried that I'd give away another penalty or be sent-off. I respected his decision to keep me on the bench, but as our defence continued to leak goals I believe he was cutting off his nose to spite his face. Yes, I had made mistakes though no more than anyone else. From playing more than 40 games in the Championship the previous season I was becoming a permanent unused sub...perhaps it was his inexperience as a manager not to give me another chance

I liked Hendon, he was an honest bloke and his training was enjoyable. I'm not sure if I would ever have played for Orient again had he remained in charge. He came to the training ground on the Monday, two days after his dismissal following the home defeat by Exeter City, to say his goodbyes.

I looked him in the eye, shook his hand and wished him the very best for the future. Regardless of how things turned out I will always be grateful that he gave me a two-year contract after I was released by Millwall.

33

I miss my mum every single day

Time does not heal the pain

I thought about this chapter for a long time, asking myself if it would be right to share such personal details. I had to consider whether my family would want it written and, more than anything, would it upset my dad? With all these factors taken into account, I made the decision that I should tell my whole story as honestly as I could.

M Y MUM, Elizabeth, was nine when she was knocked down while running across a road to the shops in Wexford, Ireland. She was dragged for a quarter of a mile by the car before the driver realised something was happening and stopped.

She was rushed to the nearest hospital in County Wexford and subsequently transferred to the Cappagh Hospital 80 miles away in Dublin. It was there that she spent two years undergoing multiple operations to save her right leg as well as having skin grafts on her face.

They successfully managed to save the leg, but because of the initial damage caused by the accident it ended up shorter than the other.

This led to a life of further surgery, a major back operation and a cocktail of medication.

The hospital was a long way from home and it was difficult for family and friends to visit. As well as her physical injuries, the accident left mum mentally scarred. Spending so much time in hospital meant she had little or no secondary education. It was an incredible amount for someone so young to go through.

She underwent three hip operations by the time she was 39. She had pins and plates in her legs plus scars on her hip which were a permanent reminder of her awful ordeal. There was a trayful of prescribed tablets and pills to take each day to help her, but the pain and the huge amount of medication along with the inevitable pressure of bringing up five children on a limited budget unsurprisingly started to affect her.

Mum turned to drink as a way to ease her depression and pain. Alcohol became a habit which did not help her condition or mental state, especially while on heavy medication. She was registered under a number of doctors both at the hospital and at her surgery, each with a different opinion and concern.

Her back pain became so severe that she was prescribed morphine prior to her operation and having gone nil by mouth twice, expecting her operation to take place, she was sent home after her intended surgeon was redirected to fatal car accidents or other serious demands.

Eventually she had the back operation she had been waiting for. Following the surgery she was prescribed a variety of medication including morphine, cyclizine, tramadol, diazepam and Di Hydro codeine.

I cannot remember a day when mum was not in considerable pain.

$$* \quad * \quad * \quad * \quad *$$

WHILE I may sound more south London than Dublin I am very much Irish through and through. It was June 1984 when my mum, dad, older brother Paul and I came over from the Irish capital to Crewe. Dad was looking for work, mum was pregnant with her third child and jobs were becoming harder to find.

Life was not easy for the Dunnes and it became even more of a challenge.

Within a few days of my brother being born, mum and dad decided to head to London to stay in my aunt's house. Dad eventually found work and it was from this job that we managed to move into a flat in Avondale Square on the Old Kent Road.

Later, dad took a job managing a pub in Hoxton where we lived for two years before it was sold, rendering us homeless.

We ended up in a number of B&Bs in Paddington. This was an extremely difficult time for the family as two more sisters had been born and there were now seven of us.

After living at a friend's house for a short while, we qualified for a run-down fourth-floor flat in Hornsey, north London. The block had no lift and we had to step over people shooting up on the stairwells.

Living there, not least having to walk up and down so many steps, caused further damage to mum's disability. After several months in a place that was like a set from *Breaking Bad*, we became eligible for a three-bedroom flat on the infamous

Bemerton Estate on the 'Cally' – Caledonian Road, north London.

Anyway, after two years on the 'Cally', with mum's condition deteriorating, we were moved to a mobility unit in Highbury, a stone's throw away from the old Arsenal stadium. Here, there was a room downstairs that could have been used as a bedroom should mum become wheelchair-bound. She never did make a wheelchair; she had great fighting spirit and was determined to keep going, pushing herself through the pain barrier.

Sadly, this was to be the address of her final resting place.

* * * * *

IT WAS 28 SEPTEMBER 2000. It was around 7pm and I was playing snooker in Downham, near Bromley, when I received the call no son or daughter wants. Call it sixth sense, but I just knew when I answered the phone that mum had died.

Dad's words and tone are still clear in my mind today.

The last time I had seen mum alive was three weeks previously when we went for dinner in the old Crown pub at Bromley Common. She and dad had taken me out after I had passed my driving test and that night she was her usual bubbly self, hiding any pain from me.

I said farewell to her and after dad drove off, the car suddenly stopped and turned back only for mum to get out. In her strong Wexford accent she said, 'Alan, you never gave me a kiss goodbye.' I thought at the time this seemed a little strange. I remember all of this like it was yesterday.

I miss my mum every single day and those who say that time is a healer are wrong.

Mum's death saw the break-up of the family. She was the rock, the one who kept us together and after she passed away it wasn't long before we all went our own ways.

My relationship with my two brothers and two sisters is not as close as it would be if our mum were still alive. This is sad, but I think we just grew apart and did our own things after her passing. However, I'm still very close to dad and see him regularly. He is not just my father, he is also my best friend.

Later, dad brought a legal challenge against the medical staff involved in mum's care before her death. He hired a team of solicitors who specialised in medical neglect to investigate, but the coroner ruled that her death was due to medication toxicity and the doctors were cleared of any neglect.

Following mum's death, dad could easily have given up, not least as he had lost his mother a month earlier. Credit to dad, he stayed strong for us and turned his life around. From smoking 40 cigarettes a day and drinking far too much, he quit smoking and is partial only to the occasional glass of red wine.

As big a victory as anything his son has achieved.

The men in charge during the Alan Dunne years at Millwall

Mick McCarthy	21/03/1992 to 03/02/1996
Ian Evans	10/02/1996 to 10/02/1996
Jimmy Nicholl	13/02/1996 to 08/02/1997
John Docherty	15/02/1997 to 03/05/1997
Billy Bonds	09/08/1997 to 02/05/1998
Keith Stevens	08/08/1998 to 02/05/1999
Keith Stevens and Alan McLeary	07/08/1999 to 16/09/2000
Ray Harford and Steve Gritt	19/09/2000 to 23/09/2000
Mark McGhee	26/09/2000 to 14/10/2003
Dennis Wise	18/10/2003 to 08/05/2005
Steve Claridge	21/06/2005 to 27/07/2005
Colin Lee	07/08/2005 to 17/12/2005
David Tuttle	26/12/2005 to 15/04/2006
Alan McLeary and Tony Burns	17/04/2006 to 30/04/2006
Nigel Spackman	05/08/2006 to 23/09/2006
Willie Donachie	26/09/2006 to 06/10/2007
Richard Shaw and Colin West	13/10/2007 to 06/11/2007
Kenny Jackett	10/11/2007 to 04/05/2013
Steve Lomas	05/06/2013 to 26/12/2013
Neil Harris and Scott Fitzgerald	27/12/2013 to 06/01/2014
Ian Holloway	06/01/2014 to 10/03/2015
Neil Harris	10/03/2015 to present

(Source: www.millwall-history.co.uk)

Millwall's all-time record appearances

1   **596** Barry Kitchener (1966–82)

2   **557** Keith Stevens (1980–99)

3   **443** Harry Cripps (1961–74)

4   **431** Neil Harris (1998–2004, 2007–11)

5   **413** Alan McLeary (1981–93, 1997–99)

6   **388** Alan Dunne (2000–15)

7   **361** Paul Robinson (2001–15)

8   **343** Jim Forsyth (1929–39)

9=   **341** Richard Hill (1919–30)

9=   **341** Len Graham (1923–34)

Index

Index